T·H·E
LYNCH MOB

T·H·E
LYNCH MOB
Stringing Up Our Prime Ministers

CHARLES LYNCH

KEY PORTER·BOOKS

Canadian Cataloguing in Publication Data

Lynch, Charles
  The Lynch mob

ISBN 1-55013-108-7

1. Prime ministers – Canada. 2. Prime ministers – Canada – Public opinion. 3. Press and politics – Canada. I. Title.

FC600.L85 1988   971.06   C88-094335-1
F1034.2.L85 1988

The publisher gratefully acknowledges the assistance of the Ontario Arts Council.

Key Porter Books
70 The Esplanade
Toronto, Ontario
Canada M5E 1R2

Printed and bound in Canada by
T. H. Best Printing Company Limited

88 89 90 91 92 6 5 4 3 2 1

Contents

The second oldest profession is either politics or journalism. Each has more lay experts than the oldest profession. This book is for them.

"Bare your navel!" – *Mrs. Peter Lougheed to Charles Lynch, 1975*

(I bared it, and she thumbed a rhinestone into it, and to the best of my knowledge, it's still there.)

T·H·E
LYNCH MOB

"Who Elected You?"

"The press calls itself a bridge between Parliament and the people. Barrier I call it."
                                                    – *Pierre Trudeau*

Four of the ten prime ministers I have reported on are still alive and well: Mulroney, Turner, Clark, and Trudeau.

Four at one time has happened only twice before, when Borden, King, Meighen and Bennett were on the hoof, in the 1930s. During the 1960s there was a spell when Pearson, Diefenbaker, St. Laurent and Trudeau were all alive, each ignoring the existence of the others.

All the prime ministers have cursed the country's complexities in private, while counting its blessings in public. And all have damned people like me, whose reports and commentaries, written and spoken, have helped shape the public's impressions of them and their work, usually bending the issues out of shape in the process.

I have known prime ministers, as much as scribes ever know

them, from my days as a young reporter, through columnist and pundit and finally, I suppose, sage. I passed from a knowledge of Meighen and Bennett to an awe of King, to a respect for St. Laurent, admiration of Diefenbaker, affection for Pearson, astonishment at Trudeau, sympathy for Clark, rejection of Turner and joy followed by despair for Mulroney.

As all reporters must, I carry a load of prejudices and biases along with me – being a New Brunswicker was enough to ensure a full bag of those – and they shaped and shaded everything I wrote and said. For most of a happy and profitable time I was paid to unload my own slant on things to the buying public.

The early years were straight reporting, or that's what we called it before we and the public came to realize there could be no such thing.

With this hard-news background, hammered into me by years in the trenches of three of the toughest news agencies – Canadian Press, United Press and Reuters – I turned to column writing in 1962, in time for the Diefenbaker-Pearson transition. I became first a PM watcher, then a critic, in the forefront of what has become a media pack spouting its judgments from the Hill.

And always, during this last quarter century of personal journalism (labeled "comment" but often splashed across the front page), there has been the question:

"Who elected you?"

Prime ministers ask the question – it was a favorite jibe of Trudeau's – and it often comes from Mulroney in his frequent moments of exasperation.

The answer to the question is "Nobody."

Elected news reporters wouldn't be worth a damn.

Elected columnists and commentators would be just as bad – unable to write readable stuff and preoccupied with the need to please that squeezes the guts out of politicians.

The press is impelled by curiosity, and the more curious we get, the better it is for the public. And if that means probing the private lives of public people, so be it.

The parameters have broadened in our age of disrespect to

include every aspect of a politician's life. But it wasn't so in other times. Look what Mackenzie King got away with, running the country out of a crystal ball and the alignment of the hands on the clock, seeking inspiration amid his phony ruins at Kingsmere.

We didn't know about all that until King had joined his legion of spooks in the great beyond, where he had done his utmost while on earth to prepare his own place, not to mention that of his dog.

I have frolicked in those ruins on many a moonlight night, it being the custom of Kingsmere natives to thump the hollow ground inside the stone enclosure at the midnight hour, challenging Willie to show himself. We have pretended to receive answers, amid the hooting of owls and the howls of feigned wolves, while perched on jagged hunks of the old British House of Commons, imported by King after the London blitz to add a touch of class to his rubble.

If King could hide all these massive stimulants to his spiritualism, then what might other leaders be concealing? Had we probed King, the voters of his day might have learned something to their advantage and tossed him out.

Thus we vowed, on discovery of the ruins, that nobody as nutty as King should ever govern Canada again untroubled by publicity.

No prime minister so secretly odd has existed since, though John Diefenbaker put heavy strains on our energies and our credulity. Was Dief really going around the bend in his last year as prime minister? Who should get the net if he was? Did he really have Parkinson's disease? Had he been a member of the Ku Klux Klan during its big run in Saskatchewan in the 1920s? Why did he come home from England during the First World War, without seeing combat?

What was Lester Pearson's relationship with Herbert Norman, our Communist diplomat who committed suicide in Cairo after the McCarthyites got on his tail? Cries of "smear" put us off that trail, and to this day the mystery persists of just how deep the Soviet intrusion was into our golden age of diplomacy in the 1940s and the 1950s.

More cries of "smear" kept us off Pierre Trudeau's trail when he burst into public life in his middle years, his past a muddle of visits to Moscow, Cuba and Red China and blackballings by Cardinal Léger and bans at the United States border. We pressed, suspecting yogi connections as weird as King's adventures in the occult, but Trudeau stared us down and scared us off. We still don't know even the half of it.

We did our best to expose the tendency of prime ministers to accept hospitality from the wealthy seeking government favors. Diefenbaker did it, and Pearson did it, and Trudeau did it, and the only emotion they showed when the vacation visits became public knowledge was indignation at the press for implying that they could be bought by a visit.

When Brian Mulroney goes to Palm Beach in Florida on holiday, we are never sure where he's staying, or with whom, though we are assured by his staff that everything is above board and questions about it are contemptible.

In all this we are open to the charge of sounding holier than thou, in light of the lives led by media people. But our private lives don't have to jibe with our public views, because nobody elects us – nobody would, as every prime minister has insisted ever since the harassed Diefenbaker dubbed us "the servile press."

And yes, there remains the delightful possibility that Willie King was sane, and the rest of us were nuts. Or that the Joe Clark duckwalk and the Mulroney glide are normal and everybody else is out of step. Likewise Pearson's shuffle and lisp, and Diefenbaker's trembles. Does Turner really drink a lot and smack his lips? And did Trudeau pirouette after yoga exercises on the dining-room table?

When our critics persist, I ask if they would prefer their political reporting through government sources, in which case dozens of countries await them where things are done that way.

Would they rather live in Beirut, or perhaps Belfast?

Fifty-two years of watching politicians and writing about them and commenting on their lives and works have taught me a few things about Canada and its leaders, and I want to share some of that with you in this book. They have also taught me that pundits can get more puffed up than politicians, with far less to get puffed up about. Our lives tend to be more messy, less grandiose than the lives of those we criticize.

Stanley Knowles and I are the only ones still on The Hill from the first parliament I covered in 1947. Today he has an honored place in the House of Commons; I don't even have a desk in the Press Gallery to call my own. So be it.

Yet my job is as fascinating as it was when I was writing about Bennett, or King, or St. Laurent, or the men who kept the place in constant ferment – Diefenbaker and Pearson, Trudeau and Clark, Turner and now Mulroney.

The relationship of the press and the prime minister remains as elusive as Willie King's ghost, though those spook parties continue by the light of the Kingsmere moon. Great fun they are, too. And so, I admit, is this questionable business of reporting and commenting on what has to be the most impossible job in Canada.

1. The Me in Media

"The Press Gallery is an adjunct of Parliament."

– Pierre Trudeau

In October 1935 my home-room teacher at Saint John Vocational School despaired of my marks in every subject except English and typing.

Accordingly, he arranged for me to write a sports column in the school paper, the *Challenger*, and suggested I get some sort of grounding in politics, starting with an upcoming Tory rally that would be addressed by Prime Minister R.B. Bennett. "A special assignment," he called it.

I protested that I wanted to be a sports writer, a lasting ambition that I achieved only in my cub reporting days when a reporter covered everything from police court to the Grey Cup.

But I went to the rally.

I was fifteen at the time, and something Bennett said that day made an indelible impression on me. He told us that, at age sixteen, he had graduated from the provincial normal school in Fredericton, almost half a century earlier. His message was clear: young men from New Brunswick could make good, just as he had.

Almost 4,000 people were at the meeting. It was late in the campaign, and Bennett's voice was husky, but still he worked his way through what I would later come to know as a gasser. Speeches were expected to amount to something in those days, and Bennett brought loud cheers when he said, "The Liberals are in full flight, they are routed."

When he was asked about restlessness in relief camps – the original work-for-welfare projects – his reply was that men got twenty cents a day spending money, plus food, shelter and work clothes, "and that was more than most of them were entitled to." Then he added that as a successful man of wealth he had no reason himself for pursuing a strenuous life "except that Canada made possible my success, and I owe a debt to my country that I must try to pay."

The following week the voters of Canada relieved Bennett of that obligation. But in his speech to us in Saint John he had shown no sign of knowing that the wheels had fallen off. He'd ridiculed the Liberal claim that his Tories would win only forty-five seats.

In fact, the Liberal estimate was six seats high.

What I retained most forcefully from Bennett's speech was that New Brunswickers could get rich by leaving. Much later I heard a distinguished judge in Regina put it another way: "The smart ones all come from New Brunswick, and the smarter they are, the quicker they come."

So it was that a prime minister set me on my path in life.

Growing up in New Brunswick between the wars, I was not particularly aware of national politics, but I did notice that my engineer father seemed to be in or out of work depending on which party won power in the province. Father's steadiest job came when they started paving the roads in the mid-1930s. By that time I was at work on the local paper – age sixteen, earning seven dollars a week – a happy, carefree product of the Depression. (Like the joy of war, it is impossible to explain to later generations.) I had no set beliefs, but I had an inkling that if this was not yet the best of all possible worlds, it was sure to get there.

The Depression spawned radical political parties elsewhere, but in New Brunswick political protest seemed foreign. Our big preoccupation was how to keep food on the table, and fear of getting fired has stayed in our subconscious to this day, along with a distaste for bread and molasses. (Most of us also resolved never to go to war; most of us went when the time came and counted it an adventure.)

It was 1947 and I was twenty-eight when I started reporting on Canadian national politics from Ottawa, after twelve years of police court, reporting on the action at local hotels and city hall, the war, the Nuremberg trials and the emergence of the Third World. (I worked in Latin America for a spell.)

After witnessing the end of the King era in Ottawa and the start of the St. Laurent decade, I became a foreign correspondent in my native United States and took a long firsthand look at American politics and world diplomacy at the United Nations. In 1958 I opted to return to Ottawa just when Canadian politics turned exciting with the emergence of John Diefenbaker.

I have tried through the years to nourish the belief that elected office is the highest calling of all. My experience has been the reverse of the Ottawa norm of idealism at the start and no beliefs at all at the end.

Celebrity journalism was unknown in my early days, apart from Gordon Sinclair, who laid the foundation for his fortune by being against everything, and Robertson McLean, whose forays into Ethiopia eventually brought him to Saint John, N.B., dressed in Ethiopian costume and telling tall tales.

We did have the fabled Harold Dingman, who wrote better drunk than the rest of us did sober until he trembled too much to hold a pencil or sign cheques for his booze. I may have hastened his untimely death by ghost-writing a column under his name while he was on a binge. It was about bird-watching, and he said that when he read it it made him puke even harder.

And there was Judith Robinson, whose pen could sing, and sting.

But the rest of us in the national press corps were the very definition of uncelebrated. We worked in a crowded, cluttered slum at the back end of Parliament's Centre Block, with the fire marshal forever threatening to clear the place out. Card games were endless, and the whiskey flowed freely from the bootleg bar, day and night.

Opinion columns were unknown in those days, except for *Maclean's* "Man With A Notebook," who was eventually identified as the brilliant Blair Fraser. Bylines were not usual, and our main job was to cover anonymously the debates in the House of Commons.

I took as my model the reports of John Bird of Southam; they were essays based on the debates of the day, written in the ornate – and now extinct – style set by the quality papers in Britain. Alas, Mr. Bird fell victim to the grape, and when it became my lot to succeed him in the Southam chair, his kind of parliamentary writing was already going out of fashion. (Bird made a remarkable comeback and had a marvelous column for the *Ottawa Journal* on, well, birds.)

In the old days covering Ottawa meant staying in Ottawa. St. Laurent was our first leader to travel at home and abroad with an entourage that included the press. Reporters accompanied him by train at home and by plane "overseas," as we still called it. In the latter he was imitating his foreign minister, Lester Pearson, who pioneered the global junket with media freeloaders on board not as a privilege, or a reward, but as a right. The seats on the plane were available; somebody might as well fill them.

St. Laurent followed Pearson's world tour with one of his own, from which he returned in such a state of exhaustion that he was never the same again.

Media people enjoyed these tours immensely right up to the Trudeau years, when the media bosses – the newspaper and station owners and the upper levels of the CBC – started insisting that reporters and technical staff take no more freebie handouts. Once management insisted on paying the passage of their minions, the golden age of media travel was at an end.

In the junket's stead came the working tour, with the press corps looking to embarrass rather than publicize the touring prime minister. What the media shells out in fares often more than pays for the plane, so today it's often the politicians who get the free ride. But they also get savaged.

In the switch over a twenty-year period from cheering section to lynch mob, that old devil "public interest" has been lost, fretted over only by those who anguish over the difference between press freedom and press licence.

My colleague and contemporary, columnist Douglas Fisher, writes of "the generational tilt in the media," particularly in TV and radio "where the kids hold most of the reporting jobs."

"Their sympathies," he says, "run anti-government."

So they do, though for selfish rather than political motives, I believe. They want the news all right, but more than anything these young journalists want to be seen, heard, and read as the depicters of the news.

Maybe between the wars we kid reporters acted in similar ways. But we always lacked bylines, and any access to even fleeting fame was by and large denied. For us something about our role needed no additional glorification. Anyway, celebrity was mostly unavailable because in the social circles of the time, high and low, newspaper people were usually shunned, unless they owned the paper.

None of this is to say that the old days in journalism were necessarily better than journalism today. *Time* magazine veteran Thomas Griffith, in his farewell column, said that although he missed the rowdy capriciousness of the old reporting, he did not miss the gentlemen's agreement to censor. He doubted that today's media would have honored, as U.S. newspapers and newsreels of the period all did, an agreement never to show President Roosevelt's leg brace, or his aides lifting him into place at banquet tables and podiums.

Despite all my caveats there is much about the profession of news reporting in our present era that is a relief from the past. It is because of this that I am able to stay continually fascinated by political journalism. And I doubt that my interest will flag, provided the good changes keep pace with the ones that aren't so good.

My personal situation as a political reporter and commentator is more complicated today because I am a "parliamentary spouse."

This opens up a side of politics that pundits know nothing of, and I have been steeped in it since my wife, Claudy Mailly, became the Conservative Member of Parliament for Gatineau in 1984.

She wasn't an MP when we got together, and she wasn't my wife, either. But four years after we set up housekeeping she ran for election and she won, in a riding that had never voted Tory.

Since then she has been working in Parliament and in the riding, and eating my cooking when she can get home, and attending more functions than political writers would believe.

When people wonder how I can keep my political impartiality, I tell them I thank God she's a Tory because Tories are more fun than Grits or New Democrats. The party takes in every shade of opinion, from Claudy's red tinge to the dinosaurs, with whom she gets along just fine. But she never tells me what goes on in caucus or party circles.

Dirty tricks have been played against her, and she has learned to sense them coming. I stay out of the partisan stuff, but I'd hate to run against her.

And she's taught me a great deal about the House of Commons, things I never knew despite thirty-four years studying the place first hand.

2. The Hill

"This country was not built by timid souls." – *Brian Mulroney*

It is our hill of hope, it is our hill of dreams, some fulfilled, most broken.

Prime ministers and kings and queens have walked here. Ordinary folk come to sightsee and picnic and browse or line up for the guided tours or the trip up to the clock. New members of parliament come with wonder and high hopes, which some of them sustain, though most do not.

For me it has been a work place for thirty-four years, years of profound change for the capital and the country, years of constant animation in our politics and great good fortune for the governed.

This seat of government has been my joy and my despair, where everybody and everything seem transient, where people come and go almost as quickly as their reputations and achievements.

It is our Pantheon. It houses our Hall of Honour, in a setting as magnificent as any cathedral, used for solemn national occasions and raucous cocktail parties.

During these rituals, I have imagined that if ever there was a nuclear war, The Hill would become encased in a vast blob of melted glass from the highrise temples of commerce that dominate the scene today. Surviving generations peering into the silicone cake would ponder what went on here and what the monuments strewn about might have commemorated, much as our own century wonders about Stonehenge.

Although our monuments are not as imposing, nor as neatly arranged, our setting is more majestic than Washington's. It is less chaotic than Westminster's hodge-podge – nobody gets lost on Parliament Hill, except the occasional bear, or moose, or beaver, or drunk.

I have seen The Hill function as the highest court in the land, and as an old-style lunatic asylum cum prep school loved by some inmates, loathed by others.

Every prime minister of my acquaintance has despaired of it as an obstacle to his best-laid plans and his fondest ambitions. Each of them has strolled among the statues of his predecessors, perhaps reflecting that the most lasting thing you get for being prime minister is a statue on Parliament Hill, amid the demonstrators, marchers, protesters, tourists, and embracing lovers.

And pigeons. In summer's heat or winter's blast the pigeons deposit upon our prime ministerial images, from the top down. A prime minister might muse that the voters have done this for years.

Come for a stroll around the place. It is the most noble setting for a seat of government in the world, with its view of natural wonders to the north, the surging Ottawa River and the Gatineau Hills beyond, and in the foreground the man-made marvels of the 1980s – the museums of art and civilization, plus three billion dollars' worth of federal office buildings on the Quebec side of the river.

It is appropriate that the biggest statue on The Hill is of Queen Victoria, for it was she who chose the site as a compromise between the ambitions of Toronto, Kingston, and Montreal. (We still celebrate her birthday as the opening of the fishing season.) Victoria is the only ruler commemorated on The Hill, though a statue is on the way of Elizabeth II, a frequent visitor to the precincts who has pronounced that, "I, together with your Senate and your House of Commons, constitute the Parliament of Canada."

Since Her Majesty rode a Canadian horse on so many state occasions in London, the beast might make it with her to The Hill, in bronze, giving the capital its only equestrian statue. (Toronto picked up an old statue of Edward VII, mounted, when India was cleaning house.) At least one horse permanently installed on The Hill, apart from those ridden by scarlet-coated Mounties during the tourist season, would ensure the immortality of that often-remarked parliamentary fixture: the horse's ass.

At Queen Victoria's feet there is a splendid bronze lion, carved – in the interests of decency as perceived in 1900 – with no balls.

None of the statues on The Hill includes a depiction of vitals, thus putting Winnipeg one up for its explicit rendering of Louis Riel, a statue considered so daring that they had to build a wall around it.

Victoria is not a classic; you have to go inside the Parliamentary Library for that, a marvelous marble of her, worthy of that most handsome of buildings. It is one of the four best sculptures on The Hill, the others being the Galahad at the Wellington Street front gate, the First World War soldier by the great Tait Mackenzie in the Commons foyer, and the bust of Ellen Fairclough in the Commons speaker's corridor.

There is considerable grovelling in 19th-century statuary, and some of it could cause trouble in today's milieu, as witness Samuel de Champlain, on his bluff looking across to Parliament Hill, holding his astrolabe upside down while a native Indian looks up at him in abject adoration. If I were an Indian, I'd do in Champlain, though I might first deal with that feathered landmark outside the National Assembly in Quebec City: the *porte aux sauvages*.

Victoria's lion has a forepaw on a flag that may be the flag of France, and she carries a scroll with the legend: "Constitutional Liberty."

Beneath Victoria is a bronze replica of a *fasces*, insignia of the magistrates of ancient Rome that became the symbol of Benito Mussolini's movement and the origin of the word fascist. This ancient bundle of rods bound together, with the blade of an axe projecting, was intended as a symbol of law and order, those qualities supposedly so dear to Canadian hearts. The *fasces* on The Hill survived despite becoming the symbol of violence in putting down opposition...and of atrocities, of course.

The statue of Sir John A. Macdonald depicts him with a seated woman at his feet, a furled flag, a coat of arms, and the words "Consolidation of British North America." In his hand are a pair of spectacles with real glass lenses. (Remarkably, the glass has remained unfouled by pigeons through the years.) Not a bottle in sight, though occasional pranksters leave empties here, as they do on Scottish feast days at the statues of Robbie Burns in Halifax and Fredericton.

Alexander Mackenzie is shown stern-faced, with yet another woman standing below, and a male figure lying at *her* feet. Mackenzie carries a book labelled "probity," a scroll proclaims that "duty was his law, and conscience his ruler." A plaque added later to mark the onset of bilingualism reiterates the message in French.

The missing PMs on the lawns and amid the shrubs are Abbott, Thompson, Bowell, and Tupper of the early bunch; Meighen and Bennett from the middle years; and the ones who are still walking around. Abbott and Tupper don't even rate paintings inside the Centre Block.

The statue of Laurier has a fine view of the hotel named after him, and is the favorite perch of the eternal pigeons, whose loft is the tower of the West Block. (Almost thirty years ago it was knee-deep in dung. Sir Wilfrid gets a periodic clean, and the joke has it that a reporter asked Laurier for a comment on today's affairs from beyond the grave. His reply: "I hate pigeons."

The most grotesque statue on The Hill, hidden behind the East Block, bears the mark of the "Modern Art Foundry, New York." From the futurist look of the thing, the foundry must have deduced that King was from another planet. Mackenzie King was many things, but this statue fails to convey any of them. What it does convey has nothing to do with the man whose homely face validates the $50 bill, on the flip side of the RCMP musical ride.

Apart from the phony rendering of King, the only PM's statue that is truly heroic is Len Mol's Diefenbaker. The work is so masterful that even those who hated Diefenbaker marvel at it. Mol shows Diefenbaker in characteristic pose, half defiant, half dominant, with a copy of the Canadian Bill of Rights under his arm and the look of eagles in his eyes.

No sculpture of Pearson will ever be match for this, because Pearson was incapable of striking an attitude and had no sense of occasion. A statue of Pearson has yet to be commissioned, but the best any sculptor could do would be to show him in his "aw, shucks" mode, hands in pockets, like cowboy humorist Will Rogers. Pearson's most distinctive characteristic was that he listed from side to side when he walked, as difficult to catch in bronze as his lisp.

Some of the most remarkable statues are of men who didn't make it to the prime ministership but who nourished high hopes for the nation they helped to found.

The unsuccessful melding of Upper and Lower Canada is marked by a kind of high altar in the shrubbery, on which stand Robert Baldwin and Louis-Hippolyte LaFontaine, inscribed respectively "Upper Canada 1848" and "Lower Canada 1851."

The whole thing was erected in 1913 "by the Dominion Government." The space behind this monument is a trysting place for lovers trying for a more successful union than that of the two Canadas. This spot replaced the lovers' lane that used to encircle The Hill, where footpads molested passersby as lovers molested one another. It has been said that the two greatest losses to present-day Ottawa are the closing of this cliffside path and the smell of the old Eddy toilet-paper mill across the river.

The statue of Thomas D'Arcy McGee, the silver-tongued orator of Confederation, looks across to Hull, a seated woman at his feet. A document in his hand is labeled "Confederation," although McGee was not on hand for the nation-founding ceremonies – he was in Rome, convincing the Vatican to keep Montreal's St. Patrick's Parish in the hands of the Irish Catholics and thereby repulsing a threatened French takeover. McGee was shot by a fellow Irishman the following year, making him our only political martyr, unless you count Louis Riel and Pierre Laporte. The downtown site of McGee's murder is marked by a plaque and a "speakers' corner," to encourage uninhibited expression of opinion, but it serves chiefly as a place to eat fried chicken from the emporium next door.

Back on The Hill, George Brown, editor of the Toronto *Globe*, stands high on his plinth, while a worker crouches below doffing his hat and fingering a sheathed sword. A scroll proclaims: "Government by the people. Free institutions. Religious liberty and equality. Unity and progress of confederation."

And then there is Sir George-Etienne Cartier, carrying a document marked "Constitution, 1867" with an excerpt from the parliamentary debates: "*le gouvernement est d'opinion que la confédération est nécessaire.*"

Cartier's statue is the only one on The Hill that had French words inscribed on it from the start; the others had them added later, even to the "A/TO" freshly inscribed on McGee. The effect, far from being impressive, is rather like what happened in the memorial chamber of the Peace Tower, where the words of John McCrae's poem "In Flanders Fields" had been carved into the marble. Some latter-day bureaucrat decreed that, as everything had to be in both languages, a French translation ought to be made, and there it is, inscribed in the stone, but as little known as the French words to "God Save the Queen." Even the cornerstone of the Parliament buildings has a French postscript.

There is no sign of R.B. Bennett; Arthur Meighen got carved but not erected, as the statue resembled more a praying mantis than a prime minister.

Also missing is the most successful of modern prime ministers, old Uncle Louis himself. The last prime minister to escape media scrums, private-life probes, and the terrors of television, the man who humanized the office after the austerity of Mackenzie King, Louis St. Laurent is nowhere to be found on The Hill.

Some twit decreed that his statue be put in front of the stately Supreme Court building, half-way down Wellington Street; and there he sits, denied his rightful place on Parliament Hill by a misguided bureaucrat who ruled that The Hill had too many statues already. He argued that Louis would be happiest in front of the court in which he spent so much of his legal career. This is hooey. St. Laurent was never a courtroom man. Agitation continues to have him moved to the immediate precincts of Parliament where a prime minister belongs, and where his successor has already been so splendidly installed. And I have just the spot for him on The Hill.

We await the statues not only of Pearson and the Queen but of Trudeau, Clark, Turner and Mulroney, who must die before they rate a carving. (Her Majesty, however, gets a bye.)

Complainants who carp about overcrowding on the lawns must not have seen the Louvre in Paris, or the halls of the Capitol in Washington, where statues stand cheek by jowl, to quite striking effect if you like that sort of thing.

All these sculpted dignitaries had high hopes for the nation they served – not least among them Victoria, who chose the little lumber village of Bytown, sight unseen, to be the nation's capital. Her hopes, as we shall see, came closest to fruition, though it took time to get the mud off the city's boots and the sawdust out of its hair.

Step inside the Centre Block of Parliament, if you can get through the crowds. (This is the most popular tourist spot in Canada after Niagara Falls.) There, on the stone-hewn walls of power, are the portraits in oils.

In the main rotunda are paintings of two great rivals, side by side – Diefenbaker, at the height of his powers, stands heroically; Pearson, seated, looks mousy.

Prime ministers have to be dead to get their portraits hung, but speakers of the House of Commons and Senate get painted while still alive. The best of the Commons speakers, in oil, is Roly Michener by Cleeve Herne, who also did the Diefenbaker painting.

The Senate speakers are a gloomy-looking lot, notable only for the way their eyes follow you as you walk along their corridor. A breath of spring in the gloom of the Upper House is the marvelous rendering of Renaude Lapointe, a Tarnowska fantasy that reflects the personality of this still-sprightly one-time journalist.

Every speaker gets a painting, and the halls are lined with them. Eugene Griffin of the *Chicago Tribune* wanted to remove the nameplates to see (a) if anybody would notice, and (b) if anybody had the faintest idea which name went where when it came time to put them back.

One of the many curiosities of the Centre Block is the gallery of portraits of British prime ministers, a relic that nobody has the nerve to take down. The etchings and photographs line the top-floor corridor leading to the Parliamentary Restaurant, whose celebrity has dulled since prices went up and quality went down.

Here are the faces of every British PM from Sir Robert Walpole, the man whose record in office Mackenzie King exceeded after two hundred years, to Edward Heath, dated 1970-74. There is no sign of, nor wall space for, Harold Wilson, James Callaghan or Margaret Thatcher. Pity, especially since Maggie used our House as her own sounding board, as Churchill had before her.

The Senate, in its new grandeur, decreed that portraits of its leaders be hung in the halls and created as unremarkable a gallery as can be found anywhere. But the Senate does have custody of the biggest oil paintings in the land, those of past British kings and queens. That of Victoria was rejected for display in London because a trick of perspective seems to give her a foreshortened arm. It's worth a look if only for that strange effect. The Senate chamber itself is lined with vast paintings of the First World War – there was no place else to put them. Done in pastels, they are quite restful, provided you ignore the subject matter.

Casual carvings of unofficial residents of The Hill exist all over the Parliament buildings, the work of playful sculptors who grew weary of doing anonymous gargoyles. Sculpted heads of journalists Grattan O'Leary and Arthur Ford are outside the Commons reading room, above the souvenir stall. I am one of the comic figures below the main Senate staircase, carved forty years ago by a winter-weary sculptor with a quota of faces to fill; I am wearing a tuque and smoking my pipe.

Sir Wilfrid Laurier's prediction that the twentieth century would belong to Canada has come true. We enjoy all the delights of life in the best American and European and Japanese fashions, with few of the responsibilities.

The last Canadian election decided by economic conditions took place in 1935. Subsequent elections have been about everything but the economy. Canada's standard of living has continued to improve no matter what party happened to be in power. Our socialist party has turned itself into a middle-class party like the others, and doesn't mention class at all. Who's to say that our good times would not continue even if the Rhinos were in power?

Prosperity is the great leveler, and prosperity heightens every Canadian's self-interest and preoccupation with personal well-being, often at the expense of community interests. Prosperity even overrode the one great crisis in the modern Canadian nation: the debate on Quebec separatism. Quebeckers preferred a share in prosperity to independence.

Canadians have been on a fifty-year spending spree with scarcely a letup. There is always the possibility of a downturn in the western or global economies that would take our prosperity with it. But the greater likelihood is that, whatever the prime minister's battles in the budgetary labyrinth, however great the impotence of Parliament, whatever the threat of growing regional and provincial empires, our way of life will still show the sure and steady improvement that it has shown ever since the hardships of the nation's beginnings.

There is one problem in this most prosperous of nations, however, that none of my prime ministers has been able to deal with. The injustice of the lot of Canada's Native peoples has caused every national leader since Diefenbaker deep anguish. And the only way our prime ministers have been able to come to terms with the problem has been to put it out of their minds.

Pierre Trudeau offered the Native peoples complete equality in Canadian society, but they saw the trick and turned it down. They demanded that equality be on their own terms and that solutions be reached within their own community, a community now more populous than when the white man came.

Our Native peoples have been misled by years of federal platitudes, expressing a sympathy that does not exist and goals that are too unrealistic to be attainable. Well-meaning whites who have fueled the expectations of Native groups through the years have done the Native peoples a disservice, and their hearts have been broken along with those of Native leaders.

The image of Indians in our society is of a victim race forever drifting beyond the furthest fringes of privileged society – except when the TV cameras find representatives at federal-provincial summits, where amid clouds of smoke from a peace pipe whose symbolism none of the white men believe in, premiers and prime ministers all resolve to do much, much better.

Our Indians are survivors of a brave and intelligent people, now almost entirely reduced to congenitally self-perpetuating, soul-destroying welfarism. They have been robbed, cheated and bullied out of land claims granted by solemn treaties whose authors hoped the Native peoples would disappear from the face of the earth, as they did in front of the hunters' bullets in Newfoundland.

There is no doubt that Canada is a brave and intelligent country, but I cannot give you any details of recent history, or share any anecdotes that highlight our prime ministers' sagacity in dealing with this issue, because nothing any of them has done amounts to a hill of beans.

3. Take This Job...

"If I accept, you will suffer enormously and will certainly not benefit from the move."
– *Louis St. Laurent to his children on going to Ottawa in 1941*

It is the worst top job in the country.

Most corporation presidents make more money. So do senior public servants. They also enjoy bigger offices and fuller lives; they take longer vacations and travel in greater luxury. High places are the cap on long and successful careers. The job of prime minister is the start of prolonged frustration, internal party strife, parliamentary bickering, and stage-managed electioneering – all punctuated by pratfalls, one's own or trusted colleagues'. PMs can trust nobody.

The right to privacy goes out the window, along with most of family life and freedom of expression. Aides manage your words as closely as armed guards control your movements.

If you are John Diefenbaker, you get the shakes.

If you are Lester Pearson, you age visibly and wonder why nobody on your team knows how to play the game, and you are told to take off that bow tie.

If you are Pierre Trudeau, you don't give a damn and do it your way, lamenting the restrictions and the hazards of the parliamentary system.

If you are Joe Clark, you are laughed out of office.

If you are John Turner, you drink the death potion left by Trudeau – in public.

The focus of power in Canada has been blurring since Diefenbaker took over from St. Laurent.

Increasingly, a prime minister has had to take account of the provincial premiers and the Supreme Court and the Senate and the disclosure laws and the irrelevance of Parliament.

If you are Mulroney, you want cronies around you to share the jokes and the jibes and the things that make for sanity – but then your pals are hounded out and you have nobody to laugh with the way you laughed with those boys who loved you (or said they did).

Mulroney, like Diefenbaker, was the victim of a huge parliamentary majority. In maintaining party unity, he lost himself and spent much of his time groping for solid ground and being pecked at by ducks.

If you are Mulroney, you find the federal trough surrounded by Grits, the accumulation of twenty-one years of patronage. You shunt them out and give Tories a turn, and the air and the newspapers and the bookshelves are filled with protests. People start calling you liar and crying havoc over the contents of your clothes closets.

You protest that it's all unfair, but nobody made you take the job. Nobody forced it on you – or on Turner or Trudeau or Clark or Pearson or, least of all, on Diefenbaker, who had aspired to it from childhood.

Yes, it broke Dief's heart, knocked the bounce out of Pearson, disgusted Trudeau, maimed Joe Clark, left Turner for dead. And look what it's done to the kid from Baie Comeau who has the magic of two mother tongues.

Yet Mulroney wants more.

Turner wants back.

So does Joe Clark.

Trudeau would take another turn, if offered.

Jean Chrétien itches for it.

John Crosbie aches for it.

Paul Martin, junior, can taste it, the taste that gave his father heartburn for those many years.

The only leading politicians who do not covet the prime ministership are provincial premiers. They know that no modern provincial premier has ever made it, and they sense that none ever will. No Liberal premier has even tried, and history makes only brief mention of the Tory premiers who did – Bracken, Drew, and Stanfield – and of the New Democrats' Tommy Douglas.

The unilinguals realize that Pearson was the last PM of their kind to try to run the country.

But the fact is, the prime minister doesn't run it. A prime minister tries to take credit and avoid blame for trade figures, inflation figures, job statistics, housing starts and other numbers on the scoreboard, when everybody senses that these things have little to do with government.

A prime ministerial persona animates the news and gives an image to an age, though that image is an ersatz distortion of reality.

They cease to be people when they become prime ministers. Moreover, the country is too rich, too well-located and too blessed with luck for any PM to muck it up or improve it notably.

4. Rank Failures

"This is no time for settling old scores."   – *Brian Mulroney*

Here is a list of the prime ministers that I have worked with (and worked on). All have failed, but some fail more than others. Top rank goes to the PM who failed least, the cellar for failing most:

10. Louis St. Laurent
 9. Lester Pearson
 8. John Diefenbaker
 7. Mackenzie King
 6. Pierre Trudeau
 5. Brian Mulroney
 4. Arthur Meighen
 3. R.B. Bennett
 2. John Turner
 1. Joe Clark

What was the question again?

The question was to what extent each man fell short of expectations – his own, the public's, or both.

By this reckoning, St. Laurent was a ten.

It's not fair, but rankings, like public opinion polls, never are. Times were so good when St. Laurent was in office, it's like saying Ernest Manning and Peter Lougheed did good work as premiers of Alberta – after the oil had gushed in.

And St. Laurent, like all the rest except Joe Clark and Mulroney, was a spent force at the end. His handlers, like taxidermists, ran him stuffed; he left office in a trauma, unwept and unsung, and largely unremembered (although Mulroney thinks Quebec city is festooned with monuments to him).

Disillusionment – their own or the voters' – is the common bond of all these prime ministers; that and their view of the hopelessness and the uselessness of the media.

I give St. Laurent the best of it because he's the only one on the list who never aspired to be prime minister and who undertook the job solely as a public duty. It was thrust upon him. That's the way he made it seem, anyway, though I guess the Tories he trampled while in office might have another view.

He presided over the industrialization and Americanization of Canada, including the urbanization of Quebec, and changed the face of the land forever. In this he shares credit with Adolf Hitler, for these changes were set in motion during the war, and it was our effort in that conflict that cemented Canada's place as a leading, if not *the* leading, middle power in the world.

My next best PM, with a nine, is Mike Pearson. He, too, left office a spent force; but he put more social legislation on the books than any other prime minister, influenced as he was by the New Democrats and the left-leaning members of his own cabinet and party.

He alienated western Canadians without ever meaning to or knowing why, and he led us into deficits undreamed of. But he squarely faced the French-English question when Quebec's Quiet Revolution brought it out from under the rug. He gave us the Maple Leaf flag. And he has my nomination for Canadian of the Century because he saved the peace at Suez in 1956 by using Canada's credentials to perfection.

By contrast, my number eight, John Diefenbaker, left hardly anything except the memory of himself, caught so well in his splendid statue on his adored Hill. He said he loved Parliament but didn't know what to do with it when the voters handed it to him on a platter. Diefenbaker could have lasted in power at least another decade, but he didn't because of his suspicions and his vulnerability.

He articulated a vision of Canada that was inspiring, and he put forward a notion of public life as a high calling at a time when it was falling into disrepute. He was idolized at his height, but he was a nationalist who collided with a wave of pro-Americanism, and a peace-lover who hit a wall of militarism, and he was hounded from office amid scenes that were almost biblical, or at least Shakespearean. Driven to the brink of mental unbalance, he recovered and outlived his enemies, becoming an aging legend, grieving at all that was going on around him, tormenting his successors and puzzling historians.

I rate Diefenbaker better than my number seven, Mackenzie King, despite the fact that Willie had a much longer run than Dief. King favored inaction over action, though he plagiarized the methods and policies of Franklin D. Roosevelt to the point where Canada passed from a free enterprise to a socialized economy while shaking the British tie in favor of economic, military and cultural comforts from the United States.

King's relatively high rating takes into account the quality of men he had around him, in his cabinet and as senior advisers, men now looked upon as creators of the golden days of Canadian diplomacy and public service. How much of the credit should go to King himself remains uncertain, just as we hold back from crediting him with the amazing Canadian war effort: the direction, the equipping and the fighting. The war brought out qualities in the Canadian character that had nothing to do with Mackenzie King, and it summoned talents to the national service never seen there before or since. It caused a flowering of the peculiarly Canadian genius for getting things done, for improvising, for bringing order out of chaos – even for harnessing English and French talents together, an achievement not attained by the mother countries in a thousand years.

Pierre Trudeau's favorite author, Machiavelli, might provide one standard by which King rates more than his seven and Trudeau less than his six: "The first impression that one gets of a ruler and of his brains is from seeing the men that he has about him. When they are competent and faithful one can always consider him wise, as he has been able to recognize their ability and keep them faithful. But when they are the reverse, one can always form an unfavorable opinion of him, because the first mistake that he makes is in making this choice."

King had some of the strongest cabinets ever, Trudeau had some of the weakest, despite the fact that his Quebec ministers were cuts above any ever promoted from that province.

King also did more to make Canada's image dull than any other Canadian politician, with the possible exception of Sir Robert Borden. He would rather dodge a problem than face it, one reason that his successors found the job of prime minister even more difficult than he did and, to a man, reviled his name. He was embittered when he left office and stayed that way until he died. I believe that Canada would have been a better place without him; but I'm not at all sure who, or how many, would have served all those terms in his place.

My number six, Pierre Trudeau, is perhaps the hardest of the PMs on whose head to hang the horns of failure. He finished his run rejected by the public that had adored him and apologizing for compromising on his beloved Charter of Rights and Freedoms and reducing it to a lawyers' delight. Yet he changed the Canadian image from King's stubborn dullness to quirky celebrity, and at least we earned some notoriety.

Trudeau alienated all our allies at one time or another; our supposed opponents in the cold war saw in him a more potent New World ally than Fidel Castro. He kept reaching out to the Soviets and the Third World, though without tangible result. The British labeled him trendy, before he got preachy and moody.

One of the many remarkable things about Pierre Trudeau is the way he fogs one's memory of the prime ministers before him and warps one's judgment of those who came later.

Did reporters really go at him with their fists, and did he respond in kind? Yes. Did he invite political opponents out into the alley? He did. Did women really try to tear his clothes off, and did he shower them with kisses? Yes and yes.

Was he the sexiest public man alive, and the most athletic? Or was he, in the immortal words of B.C.'s Ma Murray, "not strung right." That one I can't answer, even if I knew what she meant.

The olden days of the morning coat, striped pants and top hat and of the court uniform with cocked hat and gaiters are hard to recall with a straight face after Trudeau; although he did wear a silk topper at Remembrance Day ceremonies and got away with it, as he got away with everything in conduct and dress. He could wear a topper and catch a Frisbee behind his back with equal aplomb.

He wasn't the first prime minister to swear. Sir John A. had a ripe turn of tongue, and so did Borden and Meighen. Trudeau, however, refined on-the-record cussing into an art. He was the first PM to give the finger to common folk, the now legendary Salmon Arm Salute. He caused anguish in newsrooms when such words as "shit" and "asshole" were unacceptable in print; and he made them acceptable: even the *Globe and Mail* printed his muttered "fuck" – in tiny type – during the fuddle-duddle incident.

Trudeau makes the Meighens, Bennetts and Kings of my list seem pretty tame, though during their terms the country was in constant turmoil and Parliament was an infinitely livelier place than it is now. Its proceedings were reported on fully and

Question Period was a mere snack before the main debating meal of the day.

Trudeau killed Parliament as surely as he ended the political careers of two better men: Robert Stanfield and David Lewis. He did it by staying away, by shunning debates, by treating the place as an obstacle to good government.

His attitude induced Parliament's permanent impotence while constructing an American-style executive branch that has no place in our supposed parliamentary democracy and constitutional monarchy. Most pernicious of all, Trudeau left Quebec out of the constitution and then damned those who brought her in.

He experienced three decisive, if not conclusive, failures. After four years in office Trudeaumania turned cold, and Stanfield beat him in every province but Quebec, where blood ties saved him. In 1979 Trudeau was unpopular again, and Joe Clark's Tories forced his temporary retirement. And in 1984, rejected everywhere, he quit and left a tattered party to a man he hated: John Turner, who took the worst defeat ever. From Trudeau, Turner inherited a stableful of patronage and the fastest-growing per capita national debt in the world.

For all that, Trudeau was the only PM to finish his term looking better than when he started, in face and form, his supple body still the temple of his well-stocked mind. I can hear him snort with a shrug: "Some failure. . ." But my case rests. I always thought he was younger than I am and only found out this wasn't the case when he stopped lying about his age.

Brian Mulroney gets a five, though he still has a chance to score higher (as perhaps have John Turner and Joe Clark, both of whom still quiver with the royal jelly).

In full cry as our eighteenth prime minister, Mulroney's majority was so massive that it became his biggest liability: his greatest political accomplishment was to keep the Tory caucus together. We used to say that anybody who could unite the Conservative party could govern Canada with one hand and solve world conflicts with the other. Now nobody seems so sure.

Following Trudeau's lead, Mulroney formed the biggest cabinet in history, so big that it became merely another caucus. Power devolves on a single committee and thence on a sub-committee. Most of Mulroney's ministers were new not only to power but to politics, and trouble heated up as soon as things started to cook.

Mulroney savors leadership. At one 1984 victory party he said, "They want style, we'll give 'em style!" But it soon became just one damned thing after another, and the wonder is that he avoided armed revolt from within his party let alone coups from outside. The cry most often heard in the House of Commons in Mulroney's early days was "Resign!" aimed not only at Mulroney but at virtually every minister.

He was the first trained manager ever to head the nation's biggest business – the federal government. But having chided Turner for doing Trudeau's errands on patronage, he violated the first rule of good management: never hire your friends. He had friends by the hundreds, or fancied he had.

It took three years for the smoke to clear, yet they were years during which all Mulroney's main election promises were kept – and more. The economy had never been better. Mulroney represented Canada with credit in international councils, while Joe Clark was counted the best foreign minister since Lester Pearson. The constitution was completed at Meech Lake, and a free-trade deal has been all but reached.

Mulroney's fondest wish, to have John Turner as his principal opponent, has been granted. So has his second desire, that a New Democratic Party be held high in public esteem between elections. He boasted he'll have another victory bigger than the last, and the degree of his success will be a measure of this man.

A brief look at PMs number four, three, two and one in our list of diminishing returns:

Arthur Meighen was the brightest public man of his time and

one of the leading intellects in politics anywhere – according to his contemporaries, anyway. Yet he failed as PM twice.

R.B. Bennett wound up the goat of the Depression, even though some of his progressive measures have served us well, preparing for the mix of public and private enterprises that makes our economy so different from that of the Americans. Without realizing it, he was a founder of the modern Commonwealth. He was the last prime minister to authorize knighthoods for Canadians, and the only one to wind up a viscount.

John Turner was the only man on this list to have governed without winning an election or facing the House of Commons as PM. He will tell you with a wink that he was also the only prime minister to have run in and won ridings in three provinces: Quebec, Ontario, and British Columbia.

Joe Clark was the youngest Canadian prime minister ever. He wanted to be known as the Man from High River, his hometown in the heart of cowboy country, but the sitting member wouldn't move aside. Clark wound up as the member for Yellowhead and the imagery went all to hell from there.

Clark was a victim of a publicity poison that gradually kills without the victim's knowing where it comes from. Being called a wimp is almost impossible to fight without sounding like one.

In the eight years since he lost the prime ministership, he looks and sounds better. He might have another run left in him and might agree with Jesse Jackson that "God isn't finished with me yet."

Back to my winner, St. Laurent, for a moment.

He was the last gentleman prime minister. Like King, St. Laurent would never have been elected in the television age; unlike King, Uncle Louis commanded affection as well as respect.

His life was an open book; not even the grave-robbers and muckrakers of today have been able to get anything on him except the wartime internment of Canadians of Japanese origin.

That was as much in tune with the times as Roosevelt's similar action in the United States and Truman's dropping of the atomic bomb on Hiroshima. The very thought of St. Laurent womanizing or smoking dope or getting drunk seems obscene.

Few of us can recite the full litany of our prime ministers. We grant a measure of hero status and therefore memorability only to Sir John A. Macdonald and Sir Wilfrid Laurier. Yet both Macdonald and Laurier knew failure more often than success but were saved by the quality later known as charisma. Their personalities lived on after them, and not all their good was interred with their bones.

Such impressions as we have of Alexander Mackenzie, Sir John Abbott, Sir Charles Tupper, Sir John Thompson, and Sir Mackenzie Bowell are a jumble best left to scholars, though it is said that Thompson would have made a mark even if he hadn't dropped dead in Windsor Castle.

Sir Robert Borden must have done something right, since he headed the government during the First World War and we won. He also introduced the most lasting measure ever passed by Parliament: income tax.

Why are there no real political heroes in Canada?

The lack has been attributed to everything from an inferiority complex to too much drink to the effect of the long winters or summer bugs. Side effects are the dumping of the British heroes who animated our textbooks prior to the 1940s and our professed scorn for the hero worship practised south of the border.

Maybe the reason is that heroes can't co-exist with the broad streak of meanness that exists in our particular kind of adversarial politics.

Sometimes we try to polish up our politicians on their departure. Witness the theatrics when John Diefenbaker took his leave and the beatification of that old sinner René Lévesque, the moment his smoke-ravaged heart gave out.

Diefenbaker, Trudeau, and Mulroney scored great political victories yet soon went into decline. Diefenbaker's massive majority came apart in his trembling hands; Trudeau was on the ropes four years after the mania; and Mulroney found things coming unstuck almost as soon as he finished counting his seats and rubbing his hands with glee.

Our prime ministers are largely for home consumption. We chew them up with gusto and then complain about the flavor. It is no surprise that incumbent after incumbent has complained that the job is impossible.

Lester Pearson said it required the hide of a rhinoceros, the morals of St. Francis, the patience of Job, the wisdom of Solomon, the strength of Hercules, the leadership of Napoleon, the magnetism of a Beatle, and the subtlety of Machiavelli. And this was before saturation TV, the Charter of Rights and Freedoms, the resurgent Senate and the principle of total disclosure.

Some argue that, outside sports, there are no heroes anywhere in today's world and very few successes outside business and finance. But we are especially disrespectful of our politicians, and making political leaders heroes has never been in fashion.

A war hero named Ike Eisenhower was elected U.S. president on the strength of his victories in battle. The man who commanded the Canadian army in that same campaign, when Canada was the sixth most powerful military nation in the world, returned home to no acclaim and no high office; ninety-nine out of a hundred Canadians couldn't tell you his name. (It was Harry Crerar.)

Canada contributed crucially to victory in the two world wars; yet when each conflagration was over and our troops came home, we elected a peacetime prime minister who had unashamedly shunned military service. Our only really successful political war veteran was René Lévesque. He took part in the wars in Europe and Korea and then dedicated himself to the dissection of the Canadian union. When his failures in political combat were put aside, Quebeckers thanked him for trying, while much of the rest of Canada thanked him for failing and dying.

The Americans and the British make much more of the burial sites of their leaders than we do; we don't put much stock in such things.

There are relics of Macdonald in Kingston, including his early home and final resting place, but his home in Ottawa houses the British High Commission.

Laurier's early home in Ste-Lin, Quebec, is open to the public, but nobody comes. His grave in Ottawa is scarcely known let alone visited, despite its noble sarcophagus in full view of the teeming traffic beyond the gates. Borden lies equally undisturbed in the Protestant cemetery next door.

Mackenzie King's early home in Kitchener is preserved, and his Kingsmere home and ruins are places of pilgrimage and picnics. And Laurier House, bequeathed to King by Laurier's widow, is a museum with, incidentally, Pearson curios tossed in as a bonus. St. Laurent lies buried unremarked in Quebec City, but people there make a bigger fuss over Montcalm and Wolfe and Maurice Duplessis – and even Queen Victoria, whose critics cared enough to blow the head off her statue during the separatist troubles.

Diefenbaker rests beside the magnificent research centre in Saskatoon, which he caused to be built and which bears his name, high on a hill above the North Saskatchewan River, now the most picturesque urban site on the prairies. His memory is also perpetuated by the homestead shack that stands on the grounds of the Legislature in Regina; it's a source of as much wonder as the rope that hanged Louis Riel.

Arthur Meighen died in Toronto in 1960, and his state funeral there was attended by both Diefenbaker and Pearson. He is buried in St. Mary's, Ontario, the resting place of the impressionistic statue originally commissioned for Parliament Hill and then deemed too eccentric for that august precinct.

The others in our story are still available for first-hand appraisal, able to read their premature obituaries from the pundits and respond as they see fit.

Our PMs have helped make us the most highly socialized country in the western world without anybody's noticing, much less caring. It just seemed to happen like our participation in wars and NATO and NORAD and the Commonwealth and in the francophonie, too, though I'll admit that that last one took a lot more doing.

We tell ourselves that lesser nations like ours don't have political heroes, unless those countries were born of revolutions. Our struggles consist of lawyers' scratchings – on parchment with quill pens at the beginning, and on computers in the 1980s, when we seemed on the verge of negotiating the dissolution of the union by peaceful means. Yet the twentieth century has indeed belonged to us, more than to any other peoples in any other lands.

In the absence of inspiration from the top, we have worked ourselves into a quality of life envied and admired by all except those who regard us as brutes at hockey and despise us for our trapping of fur-bearing beasts.

The wonder is that though politics means so little to the real life of the citizens, we continue to pay it so much heed. It is a conundrum for which I have found no answer in thirty-three years of observing and writing about it. But Canadian politics still brings me to the edge of my seat, and I can't wait to see what – or who – happens next.

5. Media Violence

"These are the thorns in the crown which a man wears while he is in public life."   – *Mackenzie King*

The Americanization of Canada is often lamented, frequently by that most Americanized of our institutions, the media. And yet, though we safeguard our media from U.S. ownership and seek to impose Canadian program content by law, it is from the U.S.A. that we have acquired our current journalistic techniques.

Vice-President Spiro Agnew said – pre-Watergate – that the media are all "nattering nabobs of negativism." Trudeau, Turner, and Mulroney have more or less said the same thing; Joe Clark would have said so, too, but he was too polite.

Grit premiers St. Laurent, Pearson, Trudeau and Turner each received a dose of media venom, but only Trudeau was immune. He could spit it back as fast as we dished it out; he discovered that the public loves media bashing.

It was the fall of Louis St. Laurent that awakened the Canadian press to the business of breaking a government, long a blood sport in Britain and the United States. In St. Laurent's case big issues were already against him, and the media merely dramatized his bludgeoning of Parliament over the trans-Canada pipeline contract and the break with Britain during the Suez Crisis and magnified Grit arrogance from being in power too long.

Even so, because his was largely a pre-television era, St. Laurent would have survived the 1957 election had it not been for the campaigning eloquence of Diefenbaker.

Television was unkind to Diefenbaker's prime ministerial oratory and also extremely hard on Pearson. The studio camera turned Diefenbaker's platform mannerisms into the image of a wild-eyed, raving lunatic. Though his manner could be serious and somber, his laugh was like the whinny of a horse; as the governing pressures mounted, news audiences saw him develop the shakes, and eventually a bulletin was needed to assure the public that he had no life-threatening disease. The electronic media zoomed in on the reflex grin that Pearson acquired on solemn occasions, and it cruelly amplified his lisp.

There are few admission standards for employment in the mass media in Canada and no rigorous codes of conduct or ethics. Standards might be higher than ever in terms of education and specialty knowledge of complex fields of government, but our mass media are still perceived as contemptible by intellectuals and academics.

Professor Trudeau brought this attitude with him from the halls of academe, and it sustained him through all the years of mutual hostility that he – and we – enjoyed so much.

Television and radio and the press did not create Trudeaumania; but by depicting his attitudes and antics they gave it momentum. When he turned dull during his first term, they depicted that, too; and he was defeated in every province bar Quebec, where he was saved by Robert Stanfield's impotence in French. Stanfield's difficulties were largely media-induced, for Stanfield was a much better and better-humored man than the public was ever allowed to know.

Canadians will search their media columns and channels in vain for favorable reports on governments and prime ministers of any stripe. Each PM gets the treatment, regardless of affiliation. There's the buildup on the way to office, and then there's the teardown.

Often during the regime of my favorite prime minister, Lester Pearson, I declared a Be Kind to Mike Day in my column, only to have it turn critical in mid-flight and wind up as another lashing, administered more in sorrow than in anger. Pearson used to plead to be spared these lamentations by his friends, but we laid it on him.

My admiration for Pearson exceeds that for any other public figure of his time, in any country. His motives in seeking the prime ministership seemed admirable: of all politicians, he hoped to leave the country, and the world, a better place for his having served it.

But our job has been to turn the beam of attention as brightly as possible on the prime minister of the day, as if each twitch and twinge mattered (which I doubt); and the inevitable failings that attend every human being show up in all their distorted glory. Politicians and prime ministers cannot do without the press, and we cannot do without them; the public might be able to do very well without both.

While the list of Pearson's achievements in office is longer than any list I could make for St. Laurent, Diefenbaker, Trudeau, Clark, or Mulroney, the list of his foibles and his failings is also a long one, and I could not and would not spare him from my compilation of it. Yet none of this matters, after all, in terms of national will. Sometimes I think the country is on automatic pilot. It flies serenely on, sustained by the efforts of its laborers, its business and professional people, its artists and its parents, but not because of its journalists or political leaders.

By law, a prime minister must meet with Parliament on an annual basis and face the electors within five years of taking office; but there is nothing that compels him to meet with the media. The press conference was introduced by Lester Pearson – only twenty-five years ago – after he mastered the technique first in Washington and then at the United Nations in New York.

Mackenzie King never held a press conference in his life, and Louis St. Laurent was equally remote: reporters tried to buttonhole him in corridors, without success.

John Diefenbaker submitted to reporters' random questions so readily that on cabinet days the corridor outside his East Block office was cluttered with newsmen.

Pearson provided a special theatre for press conferences. His ministers made such heavy use of the press conference that they gave the impression his ship of state leaked at every seam.

Pierre Trudeau took to talking to the press on the lawns of Parliament, where he could count on hordes of admiring tourists to engulf him, the reporters and the cameras. Trudeau brought television into the House of Commons as a means of avoiding a face-to-face with the press. He did hold intermittent press conferences, but he maintained that reporters were crumbs and incompetents, that we needed him more than he needed us. The public applauded.

It took Brian Mulroney four years to arrive at about the same conclusion, but by that time a hostile media had taken its toll, and he lacked the inner conviction Trudeau brought to his war with media. Mulroney did try one of Trudeau's tactics when he attempted to silence senior public servants by letting it be known that anybody who talked to the media would "walk the plank," as he put it. Trudeau said the same thing; but Trudeau was a Liberal, and senior public servants looked on him as one of their own. When Mulroney tried it, the bureaucrats considered his statement a hostile act by a man whose declared objective was to reduce the public service.

So the anonymous manila envelopes started appearing under media doors, and Mulroney became the most leak-plagued prime minister since Pearson.

Back in Diefenbaker's day, changes in the relationship between the prime minister and the press had as much effect on national politics as the formal press conference. The most obvious and symptomatic of these is the press scrum, the often rowdy waylaying of the prime minister in the corridors of Parliament or in the hallway outside his office.

We called it buttonholing then, and it quickly blossomed into an institution. The entire press gallery – barely a fifth the size it is today – assembled outside Diefenbaker's East Block door, tossing pennies to pass the time while we waited for him. The Privy Council office, where the cabinet met, was almost adjacent to the prime minister's office in those days, so every cabinet minister had to run the press gauntlet as he entered or left the secret conclaves.

The initial press scrums contained no radio or television reporters. Many print people, though, myself included, did do news reports and commentaries for the Canadian Broadcasting Corporation in addition to newspaper reporting. The CBC deemed it indelicate to engage directly in the disputatious business of political reporting of any sort, let alone in the scrum.

Whatever methods the modern Canadian media have used to seek out news, we have rarely tried to plumb the depths of yellow journalism commonplace in the United States and Britain. Our reporting is duller, but we're learning. It could be that, as with our political system, we've drawn on the ways of those two countries but gotten stuck with the least effective parts of both – just as our Parliament is stuffier and more cumbersome than Westminster, and our emphasis on the executive in the Washington manner collides with our enshrined opposition forces. In the practice of mass media the result has been a neglect of substance in favor of suspicion and a concentration on personalities. We painted vivid pictures of Meighen pulling his forelock to the British, Bennett oppressing the poor, King kowtowing to Quebec, St. Laurent grown arrogant in power, Diefenbaker scrapping the finest supersonic jet fighter ever built, Pearson beset by scandals, Trudeau seeking his lost youth among the flower children of the 1960s. But we did not delve deeper at the time. For all the buttonholing and the scrums and the press conferences, for all that we did our best to make the prime minister's job so thankless, still we paid homage to the belief that Canadian reporters and their readers have more taste than people elsewhere, that they prefer to avoid the unseemly at almost any price.

Our framework of freedoms might have come from Britain and France and, later, the United States; but our means of covering the news, and our means of snooping to uncover it, did not.

The sources of R.B. Bennett's wealth, for example, might have caused him as prime minister a great deal of trouble from a seriously investigative press; but in his era a fortune collected by various and sometimes devious means did not arouse the curiosity of either press or public. Hence there was no probing into his bachelor life or speculation about the fact that a widow, Mrs. E.B. Eddy, left him her vast fortune, the fruits of which he enjoyed from a suite in the Château Laurier so large and elaborate that it later housed the posh Rideau Club. (We did have one irreverent newspaperman – Bob Edwards of the *Calgary Eye Opener*. When Bennett was company lawyer for the Canadian Pacific Railway, before becoming prime minister, Edwards was conducting a running feud with the CPR and a court order banned him from mentioning a particular train wreck. He published a photograph of R.B. Bennett on the front page above the caption: "Another CPR Wreck.")

There was a similar lack of questioning when Mackenzie King was bequeathed $100,000 by his old employer, John D. Rockefeller Jr. Reporters at the time felt it was no more than the old boy's due, and besides, it was a private matter.

The direst consequence of such politeness is that Canadian politics have long been considered boring; but behind the old gentility lay questions to raise an eyebrow or two.

These, for example:

What was behind John Diefenbaker's sudden and mysterious return from overseas in the First World War?

How serious were the youthful flirtations with Communism by Lester Pearson, Robert Bryce, and Herbert Norman in the 1920s and 1930s? Or by Pierre Trudeau in the 1930s and 1940s?

Why did Mme. Louis St. Laurent hate Ottawa and refuse to live there, and even refuse to act as hostess for her prime minister husband?

How influential to his career were R.B. Bennett's relationships with women? The same can be asked about Sir Robert Borden, Sir Wilfrid Laurier and Mackenzie King.

How great has the role of drink been in the governance of Canada? (Sir John A. Macdonald set a solid precedent.)

How close was the relationship between Lester Pearson and John F. Kennedy?

What role did Joe Clark and Brian Mulroney play in bringing down John Diefenbaker?

What were the facts about the $300,000 trust fund the Tories set up to lure Claude Wagner into the fold, and what became of the money?

Was there a similar fund for John Diefenbaker in retirement? What became of it, if there was?

Did the Tories subsidize Robert Stanfield's Quebec lieutenant, Marcel Faribault?

What sort of a man is Frank Moores, and why didn't he set up a royal commission to investigate Newfoundland's Smallwood government after he succeeded Joey as premier?

What was the true relationship between Smallwood, Richard Nixon and promoter John Shaheen beyond their common interest in the Come-by-Chance oil refinery? What were they really doing in Moscow in 1965, when they said they were looking for Nikita Khrushchev?

In the Saskatchewan of the late 1920s the Ku Klux Klan was popular; was John Diefenbaker a member?

What was the truth about the letter purporting to be from U.S. Ambassador Walton Butterworth congratulating Lester Pearson in 1963 for his endorsement of nuclear weapons for Canada? Was the RCMP report branding it a forgery really a whitewash?

What actual price do prime ministers pay for hospitality from their rich friends? (Mackenzie King accepted free board and lodging in Bermuda; John Diefenbaker did it in Nassau; Lester Pearson took shelter with the Rockefellers in the Caribbean and with the Woodwards on Vancouver Island; Pierre Trudeau took it from yacht owners in the Mediterranean; John Turner takes it; Brian Mulroney moves in the rich Canadian set in Florida.)

Why did John Diefenbaker try to eliminate mention of his first wife, Edna, from his biography?

What was Richard Hatfield really doing on his frequent visits to Morocco?

What was the real story of René Lévesque's divorce, and why wouldn't his children speak to him?

Likewise the divorce of Ontario Premier John Robarts, and his subsequent remarriage and suicide.

What was Trudeau's lifestyle at 24 Sussex and the Harrington Lake estate before his marriage and after his separation from Margaret? Was he as weird as King?

Who really paid for the Trudeau swimming pool?

What is the answer to Pamela Wallin's question about John Turner's drinking?

Did Joe Clark flunk out of law school twice, and what were his marks?

Was Louis St. Laurent really a great corporation lawyer before entering politics in the late 1950s? What exactly were his big cases?

Did Mrs. Pearson have a drinking problem? Did she have good cause?

How good, really, was Brian Mulroney's record as president of the Iron Ore Company of Canada – his principal claim to pre-political competence?

You want to know the answers? Well, you're not going to get them from me, because I don't know.

We have set in place some of the systems and practices of an Americanized press – the media scrums and the prime minister's press conference – but we have not created a powerfully investigative fourth estate. If we had, the facts in answer to that long list of questions would be available.

If the politicians had their druthers, which they don't, they'd award us prizes not for asking these kinds of questions but for asking about the economic achievements of the Mulroney government, John Turner's brilliance in holding the Liberal Party together, Ed Broadbent's talent for compromise (as in, "NATO if necessary, but not necessarily NATO"). But it is one of the strengths of our system that media can call the shots on politicians and they can't shoot back.

One critic has suggested, however, that prizes can corrupt better than politicians, that certain muckraking stories, especially those with a heavy spin, should carry a warning to readers: "Possible candidate for award; may be hazardous."

At a National Newspaper Award dinner I encountered Martin Goodman, the late, highly honored editor of the *Toronto Star*. The *Star* had won a record number of awards that night, but Goodman was scowling.

"What's the matter, Marty?" I asked. "Nine out of ten ain't bad."

"Balls," said he. "I wanted them all!"

6. Diefenbaker

"I have an uneasy feeling he is still part of this place."
— Joe Clark on the death of Diefenbaker

John Diefenbaker developed his image by knowing and using the newspapermen who reported on him. He provided the raw material, the press did the twenty-year build-up.

He was the first Canadian prime minister to prefer the company of journalists to that of politicians or lawyers. During his years as a lawyer and provincial politician he cultivated press people. Early on he established a relationship with reporters that assured him of favorable mentions in their newspapers and allowed him, over the years, to assemble a reputation that would last until the end of his days.

That early momentum eventually overcame the media setbacks of his later years as prime minister and Tory leader and helped cement his reputation as one of our greatest advocates of human rights and freedoms.

When Diefenbaker was first elected to the House of Commons, he avoided the company of his fellow Tories and instead frequented the precincts of the Parliamentary Press Gallery, preferring the antic side of life there to the parliamentary lobbies.

He was not abashed by the failure of reporters to take seriously his initial bid for the leadership of his party at the 1942 Winnipeg convention that elected Manitoba Premier John Bracken. The defeat was his way of preparing for a serious bid next time, he said.

He regularly visited the homes of Press Gallery members. He played cards with them, and he drank with them, in moderation. His first wife, Edna, became the pal of newspapermen and their wives. To everybody in the press gallery of the 1940s, Dief was plain "John," even "Johnny."

He also maintained a network of reporters and editors across the country, frequently checking in with them by phone or in person. His early speeches in the House of Commons got more than the usual press attention, helped by his advance visits to the gallery where he gave notice of his intention to speak and announced his topic and his reasons for addressing it.

His speaking style, and his increasing reputation for being an MP unlike the others, led him to be sought as a platform attraction. And not just at political events. Every kind of audience loved him, and so did juries.

Reporters doted on him, in the beginning; and when he lost his bid for the Conservative leadership to George Drew in 1948, it was a sympathetic column by Richard Sanburn of Southam News that kept him from quitting politics. He and Sanburn remained friends until Sanburn wrote a critical column about him sixteen years later and never heard from the Chief again. In the intervening years Diefenbaker would telephone Sanburn at any hour of the night or day, as he did other chosen friends and admirers. In that he was the precursor of Brian Mulroney.

As close as Diefenbaker was with newspapermen, he did not

come to power with the intense media chorus that would later hail the advents of Trudeau or Mulroney, or John Turner for that matter. In fact, few in the press corps thought Dief could win in 1957, though the media had turned sour on the Liberals the previous year during the pipeline debate.

Diefenbaker's victory was a sensation. Its newsworthiness gave a significance to the relationship between the PM and the press that prevails to this day. So direct and involving did this relationship become that it turned into one of the most severe problems in the business of governance for any subsequent Canadian prime minister.

Immediately after Dief's victory, reporters intercepted him going to work in the morning, coming out at noon, going back in for the afternoon and coming out again, then going in and out in the evening. Dief permitted it. Indeed, he encouraged it, and his unprecedented accessibility not only gave reporters a field day but increased their work load and led to the expansion of Ottawa news bureaus. For the first time there was a major news source in the capital outside the Commons itself.

The prime minister's own staff was tiny, and at that time he had no press secretary – no prime minister had ever had a press secretary, nor was there anything in Ottawa that corresponded to the White House press corps in Washington. (There still isn't. In Ottawa each and every national reporter, and many local ones, are accredited to Parliament, even though a lot of them never set foot on The Hill and concentrate on branches of the executive and other agencies in the capital.)

Diefenbaker's availability to the press contributed to his ultimate undoing. It led him to resort to "no comment" so often that a multitude of stories appeared beginning with: "Prime Minister Diefenbaker ducked comment today on. . . ." This in turn led to the mounting impression that Diefenbaker was indecisive.

His capital punishment cases backfired in similar fashion. The cabinet was the final court of appeal for sentences of execution. Letting them go ahead had been the previous norm, but Diefenbaker was a convinced abolitionist, years ahead of his time (as he was on abolishing nuclear weapons). He forced his cabinet to review each case of a murderer sentenced to be hanged, and he once kept his ministers in session for two days and nights before he could get an agreement on the lifting of a death sentence. They loved him on death row; but instead of hailing him as a humanitarian, press reports depicted him as a procrastinator who couldn't make up his mind.

The effect of these misinterpretations was compounded by a general hardening of the media toward him. When the CBC came on the scene with its own man, Norman DePoe, opening what was to turn into the largest news bureau in the capital within the largest news operation in the land, there began reporting on government that would brook no fear or favor.

This tough adversarial stance originated from the CBC's concern that the government-financed network not be identified as a propaganda arm of the government. The Tories dared not strike back at the CBC, because they feared being charged with censorship. John Diefenbaker's view of the CBC as enemy territory has been shared, of course, by every prime minister since. Norman DePoe and the CBC stars who succeeded him became better known and more popular than the prime ministers themselves.

Finally Dief appointed a press officer, the first in Canadian politics in peacetime. He was James Nelson, a respected news agency man from the Press Gallery, who knew as little about public relations as Diefenbaker did about dealing with a press agent. Nelsen was by nature a good-humored, happy man who supervised with élan such revels as the Press Gallery's annual dinner. He tried valiantly to bring some order out of the chaos of the unending corridor confrontations.

Nelson's worst moment was when U.S. President Eisenhower came to call, along with the White House press corps plus Ike's own staff, headed by press secretary James Hagerty. The unfortunate Nelson was engulfed, and his main contribution to the joint press briefings was to correct Hagerty's pronunciation of "Miramichi."

Nelson subsequently said that those were the loneliest and unhappiest days of his life.

During his later, tougher times with the press, Diefenbaker was asked for his views about some comment that I had made.

"Lynch?" he said. "Lynch! Lynch doesn't count." (At least he didn't say I *couldn't* count.) He said worse things about DePoe.

This was the man who had shamelessly chased headlines in his earlier days, regarding this self-promotion as a vital adjunct to his lofty interest in the abolition of capital punishment and the delineation of a charter of human rights. But his hunger for publicity alienated him from the intellectual élite of the land and eventually made him a target for columnists. Although he stood for the things that were closest to their hearts, the highbrows confused the method with the man, and they loathed him. (Conversely, the mass audience never shared the élite's enthusiasm for Diefenbaker's successor, Pearson, although Pearson was a folksier man than Diefenbaker, and his diplomatic achievements were more understandable and more stirring. Pearson was considered a stuffed shirt in western Canada, where voters were blinded to the man by his image as a diplomat.)

Once Pearson and Dief achieved the power they sought, this peculiar inversion in how each was perceived meant both lost the support of the very newspaper people whose writings had helped put them there. The loss of support didn't actually take all that long, for Diefenbaker or for Pearson. Their first years as prime minister were times of muddle, and matters swiftly tumbled down paths that distorted their images and wrecked their political fortunes.

The early years of any new government are liable to be chaotic. Louis St. Laurent was the only prime minister who seemed to have the hang of things right off the bat, and that was because he was playing a part that had been scripted for him in good times. He was cast as the lovable old uncle who always had something nice up his sleeve for the kiddies.

A quarter century after the Diefenbaker débâcle, the first years of the Mulroney government were like a Marx Brothers movie, a far cry from the early, memorable time of Trudeaumania. Usually, given the adversarial attitude of the media, the chance that most prime ministers will salvage their images from the carnage of their opening efforts is remote.

Diefenbaker got us all off to a roaring start, and the Press Gallery, which as a result of Diefenbaker's upset victory had mutated into a fully fledged media corps, devoted itself wholeheartedly to making the Chief's life a misery.

Some of the mileage we got from him was good humored. Concerning the disorder following resignations from his cabinet he said he was reminded of an argument among a surgeon, an engineer and a politician over whose was the oldest profession. "The surgeon said it was medicine because the operation on Adam's rib produced woman. The engineer said his profession came first because it created order out of chaos. The politician won by saying: 'Who do you think created the chaos?' "

Another time, when discussing how the Liberals had sent what they called a "truth squad" to counter him at his rallies, he recalled that he had once been greeted at a meeting in Trail, B.C., by Doukhobors who disrobed before him.

"Now that," he said, "was a truth squad. They gave us the bare facts."

He particularly enjoyed a *double entendre*. Toward the end of his life he shared the VIP cabin on the PM's armed forces Boeing jet with Prime Minister Trudeau, at Trudeau's invitation. He was asked how he felt being isolated with Pierre.

"I took all precautions," he replied with a wink.

Dief was a determined, no-nonsense man. During the 1963 campaign, when an aide suggested smuggling him from a hall to avoid an angry mob, Diefenbaker said, "I don't go out side doors." And when a protester said he was going to hit him with his placard stick, Diefenbaker glared and said, "You haven't got the guts. You lay one hand on me, and I'll give you the worst trimming of your life."

I remember a time when, after an old enemy of his had come and gone from his office, he closed the door, checked to make sure no secretary was within earshot and then said in measured tones to those present, "That man is a cunt." (I am reminded of a grand story about Sir Robert Borden who, after finding out the source of a cabinet leak, wrote to a friend: "I have endeavored with no small expenditure of time and energy to trace the origins of this extraordinary circumstance and have at last discovered the person responsible for a betrayal unprecedented in my experience. I am driven reluctantly to the considered conclusion that this gentleman is a dirty, low-down son of a bitch.")

Every prime minister I have known, bar King and St. Laurent, used language like that in private. But Diefenbaker was rarely profane in public, and never ever was he blasphemous. He hated it when we used hymn melodies for our political parodies.

One of his favorite jokes in the 1960s was that the "Pool" logo on the tractor caps worn by Saskatchewan farmers stood for "Piss on Otto Lang." But he loved even more the press corps' lampoon of Lang, which used the tune to "It's a Long Way to Tipperary":

It's a Lang way to trick the prairie,
It's a Lang way to sell,
It's a Lang way to trick the prairie.
And the West can go to hell!
Hello marijuana,
Change the wheat to grass.
It's a Lang, Lang way to trick the prairie,
Otto Lang's way, my ass!

There was an undercurrent of respect and friendliness between many reporters and Diefenbaker during the unstable times and the hostile treatment we subjected him to. But there was very little anybody could do to help him against television, which had started to come into its own in the mid-1950s. What it did to Diefenbaker's public image almost destroyed him.

Quite apart from the anti-government bias of the CBC, the cameras made the prime minister look contorted and unwell. In his final term there were days when his shaking made him look so odd that his condition was the subject of international speculation. On TV for the world to see was his lockjawed face animated only by the extreme trembling of his jowls, the flashing of his eyes, and the agitation of his tightly waved hair. When medics were asked to diagnose his condition from his TV image, Parkinson's Disease was the ailment most often mentioned. This was the year of his second minority government, when he all but lost control of the House of Commons to the militant Liberals.

Finally Diefenbaker took public note of what he called "a perfidious campaign" about his health. His problem resembled that of Sir John A. in dealing with reports of his drinking. The evidence that Sir John was drunk was just as vivid as the fact that Diefenbaker had the shakes. But with Sir John the source of the problem was known; with Dief it could only be surmised: everybody knew that he didn't drink.

"If anybody would care to match me in a medical examination," Dief announced to the press, "I'd be glad to take him on." And while saying this, he pounded his chest and flexed his biceps. He challenged the Liberals to terminate their whispering campaign. "What makes the Liberals feel so bad," he said, "is that I feel so good."

Then he quoted Sir. John A.'s own words after an 1882 whispering campaign about his health: "If I was to be influenced by the prayers of the opponents, I'd be awfully sick."

The Montreal newspaper Le Devoir had actually published a report that Diefenbaker had Parkinson's, and to counter the report, the prime minister produced a certificate signed by two prominent doctors saying that they had examined him and found him to be in excellent health.

He had quietly slipped down to Toronto and into St. Michael's Hospital for the check-up. The certificate was addressed "To Whom It May Concern":

"This is to certify that we have examined the Rt. Hon. John G. Diefenbaker at regular intervals since 1948.

"Recently, he has had a thorough examination and as a result he was found to be in excellent health. At no time during this or past examinations has there been any evidence of any chronic illness. Signed, W. Keith Walsh, MD, T. Albert Crowther, MD."

It turned out that the shakes were symptomatic of nothing more than emotion.

Yet they harmed him. At the outset of the 1963 election campaign he was asked if he would appear on television with any of his competitors.

"I have no competitors," he replied.

Competitors, and detractors, he definitely did have, and they took advantage of what they called his Bugs Bunny TV image. (Years later Joe Clark would be called Howdy Doody.)

Newsweek magazine, during that 1963 campaign, carried a most unflattering cover photo of Diefenbaker and an article written by editor Dwight Martin that said it would be wrong to dismiss Canada's PM as superficial, "because he is much dimmer than that."

According to Martin, our prime minister was "a man who in full oratorical flight is a sight not soon to be forgotten; the India-rubber features twist and contort in grotesque and gargoyle-like grimaces. . . . his enemies insist that it is sufficient reason for barring Tory rallies to children under sixteen."

Copies of the magazine sold out quickly on Canadian newsstands. At a press conference in Ottawa some of us held copies of the magazine's cover in front of our faces when Dief entered the room. He was confronted with a sea of caricatures of himself, and he did not laugh.

It was always his feeling that Kennedy engineered the *Newsweek* story in revenge for Diefenbaker's attempt to compromise on the issue of U.S. nuclear weapons in Canada. This difference between the two North American leaders led to one of Diefenbaker's last great moments in the House of Commons as prime minister.

He was responding to a press release from the U.S. State Department, which denied his contention that Canada had no commitment to adopt nuclear warheads for its Bomarc ground-to-air missiles.

Announcing the recall of Canadian ambassador Charles Ritchie from Washington, Diefenbaker said: "The Canadian government will continue to work and strive for understanding and co-operation. It will, as always, honor its obligations. But it will not be pushed around or accept external domination or interference in the making of its decisions. Canada is determined to remain a firm ally but that does not mean that she should be a satellite."

Subsequent revelations have had Diefenbaker calling Kennedy a pipsqueak, and Kennedy calling Diefenbaker an SOB. Diefenbaker claimed to have proof that Kennedy was working for the election of Lester Pearson as prime minister, and years later he told a Parliamentary Press Gallery dinner in Ottawa that Kennedy's intervention was the most blatant interference ever in Canadian affairs.

On the hustings in Saskatchewan he denounced Pearson's policy on U.S. nuclear warheads, a policy of accepting them now and re-examining the need for them later. He said it was like "a marriage with a divorce arranged in advance." He could easily have yielded to American pressures as prime minister, he said, but he accepted instead the burden that was on his shoulders – "For leaders responsible for maintaining peace, no waking hour is free from fear."

Noting that the Liberal slogan was "Pearson or paralysis," he said, "If we got him, we'd have both."

Dief's stand against Kennedy was not popular at the time. Opposition Liberals and New Democrats openly regarded Diefenbaker as a national menace and agent of the devil. After the Cuban Missile Crisis Dief's aversion to nuclear weapons became a weapon used against him.

But his lonely stand was a matter of pride with him, and John Diefenbaker was a proud man.

One of the most extraordinary examples of this quality was his decision to invite himself to the bilateral summit meeting, held in Nassau, between President Kennedy and Prime Minister Harold Macmillan of Great Britain. He wanted to make a point that the Prime Minister of Canada was anybody's social, diplomatic and intellectual equal.

Horning in on summits was nothing new for Canadian PMs. Mackenzie King, as pro-forma host, had done it shamelessly at the Quebec conferences between Churchill and Roosevelt, where the postwar strategies were put in place. And St. Laurent, by railing against the "supermen of Europe," had imposed his opinions on Britain and France during the Suez Crisis.

But for sheer gall, Diefenbaker's arrival in Nassau put him in a class by himself. He immediately poked his nose into delicate negotiations between Washington and London involving submarines with nuclear weapons. He played the role of uninvited guest with zest, sounding off in public on every known topic. The international press corps covering the summit (including a very vocal and very drunk Randolph Churchill, who possessed so many of his father's foibles and so few of his virtues) was mystified.

Dief took it upon himself to leak a $120 million aid-to-India plan that Kennedy and Macmillan had been keeping under wraps. The alarm was immediate, and shrieks of protest came from Pakistan. Queried about reports that the leak had annoyed Kennedy and Macmillan, Diefenbaker tried to blame the furor on the reporters to whom he had given the scoop.

After the summit he stayed on in Nassau as the guest of

Canadian tycoon E.P. Taylor and got in some fishing and enjoyed the last happy moments he'd have as Canadian prime minister.

Diefenbaker fed us great stuff. The cartoonists fattened on him, and he had to endure the belated Canadian dawning of the political pundit, columnist, commentator and celebrity journalist.

Increasingly he was consumed by the idea that he was surrounded by knaves, which in the light of subsequent events was one of his more astute conclusions. But his fears led to his government's collapse into a chaos of suspicion and mistrust. That atmosphere followed him right up to his funeral train, likened by writers sharing its cross-country journey to the Orient Express for its qualities of high intrigue and disputatious passengers at each other's throats.

For all he suffered during his last years in power, they were the most memorable ones, a time of Shakespearean plots and counter-plots, when he kept insisting that everybody was against him except the people, when even his advisers couldn't get his ear.

Always at his side was his beloved second wife, Olive. "She straightens me up all the time," he said. "If I lose her, I'll lose everything."

The relationship was not unlike that of Nancy and Ronald Reagan. "A little louder, dear," she would tell him while smiling at the audience. Some of us gave her credit for preserving his sanity during those years, enabling him to emerge at last in his final configuration as a living legend.

Perhaps the clearest sign to journalists that the old punch was going came at the end of the 1963 campaign at a rally at East York Collegiate, on the fringes of Metro Toronto. Student hecklers verbally roughed him up without drawing the usual replies. To the warm-up song of "Old Black Joe," the students sang "Poor Old John." When Diefenbaker said he had received his early education just down the street, a student hollered, "How can you tell?" When he boasted about 208 seats won in 1958, a voice howled: "And then the roof fell in."

Diefenbaker said: "I've been finding Canadians everywhere. . ."

". . .waking up." the voice cut in.

"My father was a teacher here," said Diefenbaker.

"He should have flunked you," came the call.

He told another Toronto crowd: "Daniel in the lion's den was an amateur compared to me."

He went out with a series of bangs, making "wonderful copy." When he finally fell as leader, at one of the most razzle-dazzle political conventions ever held in Canada, the vote on the third ballot was Diefenbaker 114, others 2,112. That was fewer votes than he had got on his failed leadership bid twenty-five years earlier, when John Bracken won and stuck the word "Progressive" into the party's title. (Bracken wasn't even a Tory, and to this day most of us aren't sure that Diefenbaker was, either.)

He took his loss gracefully, saying: "I have never exulted in victory and never been craven in defeat. I've been long enough in public life to accept the good with the bad, the uncertain with the indifferent. I've had the experience of defeat a number of times."

So he had, fighting his way from six defeats in Saskatchewan to the leadership of his party and the greatest political victory ever. And on that last night in 1963 there were only 100 people in his committee rooms in Prince Albert, and none of them was cheering.

His final great international event as prime minister of Canada had been a visit to London to become a Freeman of the City. Upon accepting the honor, he said: "No one can demand it, no wealth can buy it, no power command it. To be of London is to share in a stream of history that has enriched a quarter of the world's population within the Commonwealth, and free men everywhere."

He archly noted that his new status bound him "not to

defraud the Queen of this city of any rights, customs or advantages. . .to pay his scot and bear his lot."

Among those in the Guildhall audience on that occasion was the same Prime Minister Macmillan who had given Diefenbaker a chilly reception in Nassau and who had once been *commanded* (according to a witness) by a blustering Diefenbaker not to answer the question of CBC reporter Tom Earle about Britain's offer of free trade with Canada.

At the Guildhall ceremony, however, all was sweetness and light. In what might have been the British idea of true Canadian qualities, and reflecting his many honorary Indian chieftainships, Diefenbaker was wished "the sharp eyes of the eagle, the wariness and strength of the walking buffalo, the joyous speed and abandon of the many spotted horse."

Maybe the Lord Mayor had him right – he was essentially Canadian, and he helped the rest of us be more so, too.

The sum of his career is not so easy to define. He let the strongest mandate in our history slip through his fingers. He failed to come to grips with Quebec's Quiet Revolution and failed to realize his brave vision for the Canadian north and the Native peoples. He fought for the prerogatives of elected MPs over civil servants, and lost. He remained set in his ways and opinions.

And yet he did develop the notion of advisers in the successful American manner, in spite of being far more enamored of British ways. He tried earnestly and stubbornly to bring western Canadian thinking to bear on national problems, something for which his name is still blessed in much of the West. And he offered us a lesson never to go overboard for a politician, as we did for him, and risk disappointment on such a scale (though Canadians did exactly that five years later, in the heady times of Trudeaumania).

He remains one of the most memorable of prime ministers. His old press pals and a host of new ones gradually patched it up with him and helped him live out his life as the Grand Old Man of Parliament, to the discomfiture of his successors.

We wound up gathering around the flame again, and he fed us with pithy quotes and ten-second clips that drove two Tory leaders, Robert Stanfield and Joe Clark, to distraction, while we rejoiced.

Also rejoicing at some of those later remarks was Pierre Trudeau, never known to love anybody overmuch, but who was heard to say of Diefenbaker: "I really love that old guy."

So did we all, in fits and starts.

7. Pearson

"This present polarization of the world into two power groups is a stage in history. It will pass. I hope our planet does not pass with it."
— Lester Pearson

Ottawa mimic Rich Little, when he left to seek fame and fortune in the United States, took with him his impersonations of Diefenbaker and Pearson, which were the best in his repertoire. But when his U.S. agents heard them, they counseled Little not to try them on American audiences because no one would ever believe that anybody – certainly any head of government – ever talked like that. It was left for the Canadian mimics back home, including Dief's irreverent protégé, Father Sean O'Sullivan, to dine out on Dief impersonations. But only Rich could do Pearson properly – it was as hard to catch Pearson's lisp as it is Mulroney's low register.

I have a special place in my heart for Mike Pearson because in 1956 he saved us from the Third World War. The thirty-two years of peace we have enjoyed since then are our winnings from his peace prize.

He was the last prime minister to have press cronies. He would call them into secret conclave at 24 Sussex Drive and at Harrington Lake, using them to float his trial balloons. This was helpful to the rest of us, for the writings of the insiders told us what was on the prime minister's mind. The absence of such inspired leaks from the top has been a handicap ever since Trudeau slammed the door on all media people.

I had serious one-on-one conversations with Pearson only twice: first when he had me over to 24 Sussex to tell me I was the most dangerous man in Canada, and second when he came to lunch after his retirement to say he wasn't going to do any more interviews for free.

He was as good-natured in delivering the first message as the second. The grin never left his face.

In diplomacy the grin had worked wonders, and it was as much his trademark as the bow tie, or as the hands-in-pockets stance that disarmed diplomats all over the world and made him the one man – when the superpowers were eyeballing one another – who could produce the solution to the Suez Crisis and make it stick.

His solution was the beginning of the end of Canada's traditional relationship with Great Britain, but it was a proud moment for us, a moment we would feel again at his eventual achievement of the Maple Leaf flag. (The flag, I think, would have happened anyway; it had been talked about ever since Mackenzie King substituted the Red Ensign for the Union Jack.)

The saving of the peace at Suez was uniquely Pearson's achievement, although many others have claimed it as theirs. Without his handling of the Canadian credentials on that occasion, a deeper involvement of the United States and the Soviet Union with the warring British and French and Arab countries seemed certain.

To watch Pearson play his part night and day at the United Nations, deploying his aides like a hockey coach, analysing the tidings his men brought back and sending them out with more messages until he had the needed support for his concept of soldiering for peace – this was memorable.

There was a boyishness in Pearson that the prime ministership eventually knocked out of him, but by that time he was nearing his seventies, having come to office past his prime, like St. Laurent and Diefenbaker. But Pearson didn't sag until the day when, in retirement, he tried to light a cigar and found he couldn't get the flame to touch. The diagnosis was cancer of the eye.

We wrote about that, and he was hurt because he wanted to wear his artificial eye without anybody's knowing – more out of modesty, I think, than vanity. The cancer soon carried him off, giving him just sufficient notice to call in old friends and cronies for a last farewell.

I have often gone to his grave in a country churchyard in the Gatineau Hills, looking over the view he loved as much as Mackenzie King ever had, and I have wept quietly for this great and good man.

Some said he was too much the civil servant ever to be a good politician. They say he brought too many civil servants into his cabinet, thus politicizing the public service and guaranteeing himself weak-kneed colleagues who were out of touch with the real world. He never admitted such a thing and only seemed harassed when, after he announced his intention to retire as prime minister, half his cabinet announced their candidacies and leaked every cabinet secret they could for campaign publicity.

Saving the peace at Suez wasn't Pearson's only achievement in diplomacy, by any means. He sensed as no others had just how strong our credentials were in the postwar world. They would never be that strong again, nor would they ever be handled with Pearson's skill and assurance. Not only was he able to accumulate respect for himself, he garnered a great deal for his homeland as well.

I have often wished that the Soviets had not vetoed him when he was a candidate for secretary-general of the United Nations. I think that the U.N. would have been strengthened under his leadership and the world would have been a better place for it.

He played the media as a virtuoso plays the violin. Pearson the diplomat received a favorable press everywhere he went: in the United States, in Britain, in Europe, in the Middle East, in Asia, and in Latin America. He was a media darling because he made news and doled it out to reporters. He also asked advice from press people, and his reputation grew without provoking the jealousy of others – except for Dief who would dog Pearson's political days. It was the long years of having the press as a cheering section that made Pearson's plunge into politics so painful. He became prime minister, and suddenly all but a few special cronies turned critical and stayed critical.

Nobody called him Mike anymore, and he had to put away the bow ties and try to be dignified, but he was hurt by the things written and said about him. He had come to power with what seemed to be a strong grip on the media levers. But his hold slipped, as did just about everything around Pearson in power, including the striped pants.

This was the man who had pioneered the press conference in Ottawa, who had spoon-fed the press at the United Nations. When he won his peace prize, the U.N. media corps cheered him as their kind of diplomat.

Then, when he was prime minister, the press scrums became unendurable. Pearson quickly wearied of the twice-daily grillings as he entered and left cabinet, and he did not fancy the idea that reporters got to buttonhole his ministers, some of whom were either too ambitious or too stupid not to start a leak. He installed a press-conference theatre downstairs from his office and promised to meet the press corps there, possibly after every cabinet meeting and certainly not less than once a week.

With misgivings, reporters permitted themselves to be moved from the crowded corridor outside the cabinet chamber. (Later we were also expelled from the Government Lobby in the House of Commons; thus we lost an ancient privilege still enjoyed by our counterparts at Westminster.)

Pearson's press conferences became fewer and farther apart. While avoiding scrums, he continued to meet privately with his favorite scribes, whom he regarded as part of his establishment – the last hangover from the old days of the partisan press when parliamentary reporters wore party labels and there was little pretence of impartiality. Pearson cherished his "in" with Blair Fraser, Michael Barkway, George Ferguson and the visiting Bruce Hutchison, plus the rising star, Peter C. Newman. It was Newman's book *Renegade in Power* that set the critical tone for most of the political writing in the years and regimes to follow, capped in the late 1980s by Claire Hoy's devastating flaying of Brian Mulroney in *Friends in High Places*.

Pearson disliked that critical tone in reporters so much that he succeeded in moving most of the press off Parliament Hill altogether. He established what is now known as the National Press Building, where most of the big news bureaus are located, and the Press Theatre, where press conferences are routinely held – or avoided.

The Pearson government, with its repeated mishaps in the House of Commons, did sustain press interest in the proceedings in the chamber itself, for that was where the main drama unfolded. Except, of course, for the drama of the royal commissions into sex scandals and political dealings with organized crime, battles that Pearson tried desperately to stay above.

His reluctance to take blame for the scandals was not cowardice, as aide Tom Kent has since alleged. It was the lesson of Mackenzie King: consequences postponed are consequences avoided. Richard Nixon tried something similar in Washington and got Watergate, but Pearson made it work.

NDP Leader Tommy Douglas got in a telling crack when he said: "Pearson promised us stable government, but he didn't tell us how the stable was going to smell." Pearson grinned at that, as he always did in the face of brickbats or bouquets, great events or small, his face giving no clue to his real reactions, although he could produce a good belly laugh when genuinely amused.

Some of Pearson's characteristics were distinctly Canadian, but none of our other diplomats shared the Pearson technique for disarming others, the possible exception being Edgar Ritchie, the ambassador to Washington, who had an impatience with protocol that was famous and, though dressed in striped pants and a clawhammer coat, always looked as though he had just come in from a day's ploughing.

One person who never amused Pearson was his successor, Pierre Trudeau, despite all the evidence that Pearson favored Trudeau's candidacy. If Pearson did, it must have been because he had an instinct that a French turn at the top was vital, not because of any attraction he felt for Trudeau the man. Pearson's first choice was Jean Marchand, the fiery little labor leader from Quebec who had insisted that Trudeau accompany him to Ottawa in 1965. But Marchand mistrusted his own mastery of English, and perhaps his mastery of that other demon – rum.

Once Trudeau decided to run, he was mean to Pearson alive and mean to his memory when he was gone.

The Trudeau leadership campaign made no mention of the Pearson legacy and contained no tribute to his accomplishments. It was as though the man, my nominee for Canadian of the century, had never existed. Pearson himself, on the other hand, had never failed to pay tribute to the legacy of St. Laurent.

One reason why Trudeau behaved so unkindly to Pearson harks back to Trudeau's 1963 denunciation of Pearson for his decision on nuclear weapons: Pearson had favored their presence in Canada in order to honor Canada's agreement with the United States, then had subsequently engineered to phase them out. Trudeau's contempt for that flip-flop and for the Liberal Party that fell in line behind it was genuine.

Remember, too, that when it came time for Trudeau to make his move for the leadership, Pearson was a spent force politically. And so was the Liberal Party.

Scandals had taken their toll, and Pearson was showing his age. Robert Stanfield had him on the ropes, though Stanfield had declined an earlier chance for a quick and early kill when the government lost a vote on a money bill in the House of Commons. Had the Stanfield Tories forced the Pearson Grits to the polls early in 1968, as John Diefenbaker urged them to do, they would have won and there would have been no Trudeau era.

But Stanfield politely waited for the Liberals to replace their leader, and Trudeaumania did the rest. The Pearson heritage had nothing to offer in an election, so Trudeau turned his back on it, and on the man himself. The party's gift to its departing leader at the convention was a puppy dog, which Pearson promptly gave away to his wife's relatives.

Even more promptly, Trudeau called an election without giving Pearson a chance to say farewell in Parliament.

From then on Trudeau scarcely made mention of Pearson's name.

Ignoring the facts of Pearson's achievements in diplomacy and his Nobel Peace Prize sounds like jealousy to me, as it was jealousy that made Diefenbaker hate Pearson so. (That hatred was reciprocated heartily.)

As the Trudeau years unfolded, it became clear that Pearson's successor craved success on the world stage above all else and felt most comfortable when on tour abroad. In order to make his mark, Trudeau was prepared to step on Pearson's record.

To give Trudeau his due, he may well have acted out of true conviction that Pearson had overplayed the role of honest broker to troubled nations, or at least that the role was outdated and there was no further need of an interpreter between Washington and London. Trudeau visualized a higher and more independent destiny – what he called the Third Option. He sought to turn away from the United States in diplomacy and trade, seeking new friends in new places, not only in Europe but in the Eastern bloc and the whole of what had come to be known as the Third World; and he practically invented the North-South dialogue.

But in the end, policy returned pretty much to where Pearson had left it. Indeed, Canada's economic, cultural and diplomatic ties with the United States were closer than ever.

Even in retirement Trudeau has not praised Pearson any more than Diefenbaker did, and it seems doubtful that he ever will or even feel that he should.

But in one of history's ironies, when Trudeau made his last international fling before retiring (the abortive journey around the world to urge nuclear disarmament), his advance man and professional promoter was diplomat Geoffrey Pearson, the son of Lester B.

8. Trudeau

"It is an irony of our profession that people only really begin to admit our qualities when we are on our way out."

– Pierre Trudeau

Trudeau's first question of his aides when he decided to run for office was: "What time does a prime minister have to get up in the morning?"

The country had never seen anything like the first two years of Pierre Elliott Trudeau as prime minister.

Nobody like Trudeau had ever become prime minister anywhere. The man had style and guile and gall.

John Diefenbaker had those qualities, too, and like Trudeau he set off an election mania in his favor. But Diefenbaker exuded an air of sanctity, while Trudeau looked and sounded like a sinner.

Those early Trudeau years were the best – for him and for his worshippers and for those of us who watched and wrote and marveled with the rest of the world that Canada could have produced, much less elected, such a man.

In the past we had a rogue in Macdonald, the colorful exception in a dour sea of expatriate Scots. And we had the courtly and elegant Laurier, a civilized statesman, though he brought Canada into the twentieth century at the expense of leaving his native Quebec in the eighteenth. We had the populist Diefenbaker, but he was feistier and less fuddy-duddy in his old age than when he was PM.

We scribes gorged on Diefenbaker's traumas. And we dined out on the Pearson Liberals. But it was the first two years of Trudeau that were the best of times for us.

In those days Trudeau delighted in his work and was full of mischief. He didn't give a damn about anybody or anything. He had a short attention span and he favored short working days. At night he liked to boogie up a storm with an assortment of women who got younger as he grew older. It was the style of the man that appealed, and often it was the style that was confused with the man himself.

His way with clothes, his way with sports, his way with cars and women and deep books and deeper philosophy, his biting wit, his arrogance, his selfishness, his wisdom about big things and ignorance about small ones – this was all new in a national leader, and we revelled in it.

Adding to the fascination was the knowledge that Trudeau was a devout churchgoer. And he had a private side to him so intense that it was said he could only be truly alone when he was the center of attention in a crowd.

Those early press conferences – before he got to musing openly that meeting with the media was tedious – always drew large crowds, just as his appearances on The Hill brought the public out in numbers unmatched by any other prime minister, including Diefenbaker at his peak.

It wasn't so much that we expected hard news, it was just that nobody could ever be sure what he would say. Or do. Photographers, especially, hardly dared blink in case they missed a kiss or a headstand or a hurdle over a hedge, or one of his thirty-six completely different facial expressions (I once counted them up from assembled news photos).

In a voice more like the coo of a dove than the prattling of a politician he would disarm us.

"I'm not all that good, you know," he'd admit. "I cannot come up with fresh speeches once a week. . . .I have so much to learn about being prime minister. . . .I can't give more to the people than they give to the government. . . .I'm talking theory now, not practical administration."

We soon became accustomed to that nasal hum, what he himself called his lecture-room voice. In a scrum it was impossible to hear him, and the radio and television people had to suspend microphone booms, which have since become commonplace crowbars in our media mêlées.

The mania overrode all else, and it had heavy sexual overtones, introducing an aspect into Canadian politics that had never been there before. When people had clutched at John Diefenbaker's garments ten years earlier, they weren't trying to rip them off to get at his body. Both men and women seemed to get excited just looking at Trudeau. Women of all ages jumped up and down with joy at his approach, and there were lots of flaring nostrils and parted lips and heaving breasts. In the nation's bedrooms – those of matron and teen alike – Trudeau posters proliferated.

Peter C. Newman turned into a pom-pom waving cheerleader, and Pierre Berton let out yips of joy in his commentaries. In the universities, academics seemed to dance like dervishes at the mention of Trudeau. This was all very different from the haughty reaction of pundits and professors when the common herd flipped for Diefenbaker in 1957 and 1958.

We returned from Trudeau campaign forays physically battered. Shin guards and elbow pads became expense-account items – hitherto undreamed of, and rarely heard of since.

No politician after Trudeau has been able to equal Trudeau's first campaign arrival in Victoria, when his helicopter set him down in front of 10,000 people.

In Winnipeg during the same campaign Trudeau shared a platform with local candidate James Richardson, who told the assembled masses that Trudeau was the greatest man to come down the pike in this century, anywhere. (Richardson would change his mind about Trudeau, just as Trudeau would regret ever laying eyes on Richardson.) Seeking the Ukrainian vote, Trudeau then met with the visiting Joseph Cardinal Slipyj and bowed from the waist before him. After which he promptly kissed every girl who could break through the police guard.

I remember a young woman named Maria Swinsisky, wearing a banner proclaiming her the Aquatennial Princess, presenting herself to Trudeau and receiving a kiss. (A 925-pound steer with a grand champion ribbon received a pat. The steer later went for $1.05 a pound, on the hoof.)

On the last day of that campaign the bubbly aboard the candidate's plane was Cordon Rouge. A fine red Pommard had been standard fare from the first day aloft, when the press complained about Air Canada's native plonk, and Trudeau ordered up two cases of France's finest with instructions to keep it coming. (The initiative was actually that of Trudeau sidekick and oenophile William Lee, but, tellingly, Trudeau got the credit.)

There was champagne in the morning, champagne at noon, champagne at night, all poured to loud applause from us ink-stained wretches. When we ordered roast beef, there was the Pommard. With chicken came an excellent Sauterne.

Meanwhile, up at the front of the plane, Trudeau sipped his Perrier water and smiled.

The drive from the Ottawa airport was through streets lined with cheering people, in a capital that had never been given to cheering politicians, or even noticing them. Plodding Bob Stanfield didn't stand a chance with the media or with voters anywhere, except in his beloved Atlantic provinces where the electorate turned out to be immune. Everywhere else the mania was rampant.

Stories about Trudeau's youth that we passed on to an eager public at this time read like chapters from the old *Boy's Own Annual*. We showed pictures of him in burnooses, in turbans, riding motorcycles, shooting rapids. Our own Lawrence of Arabia, we called him. Our own John F. Kennedy, a pied piper bringing a company of young Canadians along with him. Our metaphors moved from Camelot to the Beatles.

We wrote that he was an expert parachutist, when in fact he wasn't. Putting emotion before reason, something Trudeau never did and preached against, we referred to him as the third coming, Diefenbaker having been the second.

We reported in amazement that he had gone to Club Med in Tahiti to decide whether not to run for prime minister, and dutifully recorded his quote about that decision in full: "So I decided I might as well run." We learned with equal amazement that he had booked the trip on a coupon clipped from a newspaper. (It was on that same Club Med visit that he met young Margaret Sinclair and told her to put herself on hold while he tried his hand at running the country.)

The moment he got the job of PM he headed for Fort Lauderdale, Florida, where the girls are, to ponder his first moves. We shadowed him but only got close enough to take distant shots of him at the high diving board, showing off his twists and turnovers. This sure wasn't old Willie King wallowing at Kingsmere, or Uncle Louis with his stiff-as-starch golf swing, or Dief the fisherman, or Pearson swinging a baseball bat.

One of Pearson's last quotes before the dawn of the Trudeau era was, "My wife frequently suggested it was time I started acting my age, but I never got the message." Trudeau had no wife at the time, but he never got the message, either. And when he did get married, in middle age, he became the only prime minister on record whose spouse informed the world that her husband had the body of a twenty-five-year-old.

From election day on we had to find a new vocabulary for our political reports and commentaries. And our dress habits changed. We put aside our racks of Pearson bow ties and acquired leather jackets and leather hats.

Our new prime minister enlivened one governor-general's garden party, back when it was still a formal item on the social calendar, in an outfit that included ascot and sandals. What on earth would he appear in next? A toga? A fig leaf?

The clothing industry hailed him as the biggest thing since the loom. But the hat business slumped, sensing that Pearson was the last prime minister who would favor a Homburg. Trudeau did try to make amends to the hatters with his weird magus lid at the Grey Cup game and his silk topper at the Remembrance Day celebrations, but they didn't take.

In his first winter as prime minister Trudeau appeared in a full-length otter fur coat. When we heard the price tag, we whistled. Two thousand bucks. Big money then, even though we knew Trudeau had a bundle. But we didn't know exactly how much, not at the time. Subsequent reports put it at $4 million, which would grow to $20 million in a blind trust ably administered by, among others, Donald Johnston.

Pierre did not inherit his father's roistering – Charlie Trudeau was a man-about-town. Pierre was flamboyant only when it suited him. He cut a stylish figure at Stratford opening nights, went to the post-Expo fair in Montreal just for the fun of it and flew to Majorca to play in the water. Then all of a sudden he announced that henceforth he would ration himself: it was time for retreat, for meditation. His changing lifestyles were as astonishing as his father's dash was predictable.

Trudeau called the press together three days before Christmas 1969 to say that since he couldn't decide whether to spend his Christmas holidays skin diving in Mexico or skiing in British Columbia, he intended to do both. Not bad, I thought, for a fifty-year-old, especially as I knew that he would pursue both sports to the limit, risking rapture of the deep and then altitude sickness, not to mention sharks and avalanches.

The secret as to why these perils never seemed to faze Trudeau emerged when we found out how meticulously he actually planned each of his jaunts. He anticipated every detail and devised all activities so that the danger was cut to a minimum. Only then would he be confident that his physical condition could get him through.

I asked Trudeau whether the press could come along on the skin-diving trip. He replied, "*You* can come." Then he reeled off the terms: no writing about prime ministerial miscues in the deep (we had written unkindly about his shanking the kickoff at the Grey Cup), and I would have to stay with him to a depth of 150 feet beneath the ocean.

My previous depth as a snorkeler had been eight feet. An hour later I was having lunch with Lester Pearson. When I told him about the 150-foot challenge, he said, "Of course you must accept. It won't be the first time you've been out of your depth."

Before departing for Cozumel (I had to look it up in the atlas because it wasn't famous yet), Trudeau let drop that he was finding government boring, which he supposed it always was when it was good government, like his. The largest problem of high office, really, was answering the mail.

We were afraid to ask what we should do if he dove and didn't come back up.

Fortunately the trip in that regard was uneventful. Trudeau used the diving holiday to get in training for the greater adventure of his first Commonwealth summit coming up in London.

It was on that summit trip that he slid down banisters, got the British nickname "Trendy," and took up with Eva Rittenhausen, whose father had run a Nazi concentration camp. It was also in London that Trudeau threatened to put "his" police onto our private lives if we kept writing about *his*.

Because of the life the press corps led, this was an effective threat, and for some years Trudeau was granted more privacy than any of his elected contemporaries in any democracy.

Once, when Trudeau was on private holiday in the Mediterranean aboard a yacht called the *Adanac* ("Canada" spelled backwards), a woman approached me on Ottawa's Sparks Street and thanked me for conceding solitude to the prime minister and not trying to find out where he was all the time and who he was with and what he was doing. Then she grasped my arm and blurted, "Now tell me - where is he and who's he with and what are they doing?"

We had only one clue, in the form of a telephone call from the *Adanac*, Trudeau aide Michael Pitfield on the line. It was a Saturday, when few public servants are at their desks, but Pitfield managed to raise somebody in the prime ministerial press office to take down a dictated press release. Trudeau was disturbed about the rise of violence in Canadian society as evidenced by the fact that on his most recent tour of western Canada people threw things at him, including wheat and eggs.

As Pitfield put it, Trudeau was reserving his right "to meet the people with a minimum of formality or protection. . . .Democracy in our pluralistic society is alive, but it will not flourish without the nourishment flowing from the Canadian mind and spirit - mindless violence can do it lasting damage."

To this day Trudeau's press release stands as the most remarkable ever phoned in from a yacht in the Mediterranean.

But then remarkableness of one sort or another was an endemic part of these trips of Trudeau's. As was his pursuit of privacy during them. When he headed for Spillimacheen, B.C., for a holiday of helicopter skiing in the Bugaboo peaks of the Purcell Mountains, Trudeau had the backgrounds of the other thirty-two guests at the lodge checked out to make sure he wouldn't be bothered "by newspapermen or crackpots."

The press was barred from that particular location, and we

had to take on faith the assurance of Trudeau aides that he attacked the powdered mountain slopes with the same aplomb he showed when skin diving or shooting rapids or driving his Mercedes 300SL at 200 clicks an hour or slapping a judo hold on an opponent or doing high twists on trampolines.

One fearless photographer ignored the warning not to track the prime minister's party to Bugaboo and had himself pulled on skis by a snowmobile for more than thirty kilometers to the very precincts of the lodge where, to his chagrin, he was turned back.

The only people to witness and report on our PM's prowess up there in the Purcell Mountains were a crew from the U.S. publication *Sports Illustrated*, who happened to be doing a feature on helicopter skiing and had booked into the lodge long before Trudeau had. I'm told they were allowed to stay because they seemed unimpressed with his presence. Indeed, none of them had heard of him (though the magazine's ski expert, Felicia Lee, apparently admitted that she might have seen his picture in *Vogue*).

As remarkable as Trudeau's inveterate adventuring were the statements, releases and pronouncements that issued forth from his beleaguered press aides to explain the goings-on during his travels. I remember all kinds of odd announcements during the early Trudeau years, but the one I recall most vividly was a summons to a briefing about "the weekend incident in Vancouver which led to an instrument of information charging Trudeau with common assault."

The briefing was conducted by Victor Chapman, the prime minister's chief bodyguard. (Chapman went on to greater things as press secretary to Prince Charles and Princess Diana before cancer carried him off.)

Chapman opened the briefing in the Press Gallery lounge by handing around a press release about the fight against inflation, claiming it was being wrestled to the ground.

We were in no mood for these tidings and demanded to know about that other wrestling mentioned in the summons.

Chapman explained that the prime minister had no clear recollection of what had happened in those moments in Vancouver when Richard Bruce Jenner, age seventeen, was allegedly hit with a sharp blow to the jaw by Trudeau.

Beyond that, said Chapman, the prime minister's office had no comment; he had only called us together on the topic because he was fed up with saying "no comment" about it on the telephone. And that's as much as we ever did find out as far as what transpired between Trudeau and young Jenner.

On the subject of violence I also recall the later occasion, in another place, when Trudeau was heard to tell a lad throwing wheat at him: "If you do that again I'll kick you in the ass."

Our fifteenth PM was not always so excitable. One night in Ottawa, Trudeau sat in the royal box of the National Arts Centre for the debut of the orchestra, a cultural event as big as any of the costume parties at Rideau Hall in the olden days. That night the Montreal police force had gone on strike, and the city was a scene of bank robberies, fires and gunfire in the streets. A request for federal troops was anticipated. But there sat Trudeau in full evening fig beside his date for the evening, Andrée Desautels, a Montreal Conservatory of Music professor who was a friend of long standing and a frequent travelling companion.

Dispatches kept arriving at the royal box during the Haydn "Drumroll" Symphony No. 103 in E. Flat, and when the orchestra lit into Schumann's Concerto in A Minor, Opus 54, word was carried to Trudeau that the Quebec government had requested troops. A nod of the prime ministerial head sent the troops on their way, and Trudeau returned his attention to the music, chin cupped in hand, eyes burning brightly. Only when the concert was over did he sweep into the night, cape flying, to give his full attention to the events in Montreal, where, by early morning, order was at last restored.

Mme. Desautels and Trudeau had been students together in Europe, and she was one of his old guard of intellectual women with whom he kept in touch. A month after his symphony date we were in the thick of the Barbra Streisand caper, and all other potential affairs faded into insignificance.

The weekend when Trudeau took off to New York to pursue Operation Streisand, the entire Ottawa press corps was trapped in a locked room to study a government White Paper on Tax Reform. The Prime Minister's Office lured us in to study the tax paper by sending out a matching release about a cultural report recommending movies, jazz, pop songs and psychedelic happenings as forms of cultural expression and lamenting the loss of Christopher Plummer to Hollywood and Leonard Cohen to New York.

Thus baited, we found ourselves incarcerated with the White Paper, and we missed out altogether on Trudeau's exploration of mass culture in the Big Apple.

I envied and admired the man. Still do. Nothing of love or affection, but much of admiration, most of it having to do with that early style of his. If at a press conference he bragged about skin diving and skiing, he also told us that he intended to master all 567 pages of volume three of the report of the Royal Commission on Bilingualism and Biculturalism. He was nothing if not impressive.

It was inevitable that our admiration would eventually change to the adversarial attitude. He made it easier by progressively showing us the worst in him – "the spoiled brat syndrome," we called it.

But in the first years of his regime our clashes still seemed like fun, and the problems we had with him, particularly over such things as language, had a peculiar joy to them.

When Montreal's *La Presse* published leaked excerpts from the report of that Royal Commission on Bilingualism and Biculturalism, Trudeau threatened to sue for violation of copyright on the document, claiming it as his own. The RCMP were ordered onto the case, amid jokes that if they recovered the stolen document they wouldn't be able to read it because it was in French.

Trudeau had total mastery of both official languages, and an almost complete grasp of both cultures, though his feel for the anglo fact was based almost wholly on Montreal and his experiences in his global wanderings. The anglo side of him was cosmopolitan and man-of-the-world, while the franco side was rooted in Quebec.

But Trudeau's way with the language – English, that is, and perhaps French as well – kept giving us difficulties.

During his first campaign Trudeau said that Quebeckers speak lousy French, and the Quebec press translated "lousy" into "lice infested."

In London he called us the "crummy press," and our Quebec confrères had problems with that one as well, as they did with Trudeau's opinion of Quebec Premier Jean-Jacques Bertrand as a man who'd "gone off his rocker."

In Parliament Trudeau called New Democrat David Lewis "The Honorable Stinker," and even Mr Speaker grieved. (Lewis called Trudeau a stinker, whereupon Trudeau called Lewis an honorable stinker. Lewis termed Trudeau "the right honorable stinker." Later Trudeau told us, for no evident reason, that the past pluperfect of "stink" is "stunk.")

Trudeau devoted many of his years in office to promoting the Official Languages Act, even after the costliest language-teaching program ever undertaken by any government in the world which succeeded mostly in ensuring that English speakers in the federal service speak the lousiest French anywhere, and French speakers the lousiest English.

Intellectually he drew his inspiration from a variety of cultures and peoples. Machiavelli was one such source. Another was our own mountainous and mutinous west coast; he even married into it (and into the drug culture, which he endeavored to understand, while remaining smoke-free).

He tried to emulate some of Kennedy's presidential

techniques, especially the harnessing of the nation's brainpower in the public service. Trudeau came to politics from academe, and he sought to bring some of that world along with him.

It was not the easiest period on our campuses from the teachers' point of view; students were in turmoil, faculty privileges were being called into question and some Yankee professors were being told to go home. In the midst of this, Trudeau gave the order to round up the élite of Canada's universities and bring them into the mainstream of political activity.

This summons, in 1969, led to the involvement of academics in policy-making seminars, colloquia and think tanks, which were organized to help Trudeau with his review of foreign and defence policy. Eventually that review hatched into the Third Option for Canada. The centers of action were the Department of External Affairs and the Canadian Institute of International Affairs, both providing input into Trudeau's Special Task Force on Europe. Hundreds of academics made the trip to Ottawa, expenses paid, and apologies with promises of later involvement were rendered to those who were not invited.

The most unlikely political seminar put on by a major party was the Liberal one in November 1969 at Harrison Hot Springs, B.C.

At Trudeau's urging it was designed as a look into the future. The drug society of Vancouver was well represented among the invited guests, and so were a singular number of narcotics agents disguised as members of the media.

Trudeau's big speech at the conference was about genetic engineering. To some of us it sounded like bringing the breeding practices of the barnyard into the bedrooms of the nation. The talk was of how the human strain could be improved the way we had improved the strains of plants and animals, and how development of high-yield wheat might lead to a greater control over human reproduction. Aides insisted that the PM was not talking master race, merely trying to dramatize the kind of technological questions that were likely to confront Canadians in the 1970s.

"Technology," he intoned from the platform, "is attacking human reproduction and therefore love itself, that most hazardous and least rationalized of all our ways of feeling and acting."

Conference Chairman Al Linden hailed Trudeau as "our intellectual guru, our philosophical leader and teacher."

Trudeau certainly looked the part, with his Caesar hairdo, turtleneck sweater, suede jacket, corduroy trousers and suede shoes. He told the delegates to leave short-range questions ("Coney Island stuff" he called them) for the cabinet to handle. The targets for discussion should be the underlying conditions that caused each crisis, and the quest should be for the symptoms rather than the disease.

The conference led to nothing, but it reinforced the impression of Trudeau the intellectual, a weapon he used to con not only the party but the voters and, most remarkably, the media. We came to believe that he was the leading intellectual in the land, whereas he was merely the leading intellectual in politics. University faculties abounded with minds the equal of his, but their owners preferred the ivory tower to the Peace Tower.

Journalists, members of Parliament, and business, labor and farm leaders were all left out of the think-tank process, and there were some muttered protests. But not much came of these intellectual get-togethers, and the Third Option turned out to be a ballyhooed non-starter, though echoes of it can still be heard among the Canada Firsters and the Committee on Un-Canadian Activities.

The most lasting outcome of élite input into government policy was a scheme to give External Affairs diplomats sabbatical years on university campuses, where they would meditate in serenity on the problems of the world, provided the noise of student unrest subsided. I still think that a spell in a factory or a farm or a business office might have done them more good.

In the end Trudeau abandoned his quest for anglo élitists who would match his Quebec collection and settled for the likes of Keith Davey, Don Jamieson, Eugene Whelan, and James Richardson. On the cerebral side he had always had Michael Pitfield, whose background at least was Montreal, and Otto Lang and Ivan Head, his Erlichman and Kissinger, as he called them.

None of us in media could ever understand what Trudeau saw in Pitfield, partly because Pitfield never bothered with us and consequently remained a figure of even deeper mystery than Trudeau himself. Pitfield was catapulted into the top job in the public service, and there he stayed as long as Trudeau was in power. When that ended, Trudeau put Pitfield in the Senate, in one of his many blatant acts of patronage.

Although Trudeau ultimately abandoned his leading-edge approach when it came to think tanks, he remained fascinated by computers and flow charts, and he was the first of our prime ministers to try seriously to harness modern media, even while he held in contempt all those in the media business.

He never tired of trying to do something about the CBC, despite pretending not to watch its programs, just as he insisted that he didn't read magazines or newspapers. Certainly he had the right answer to a hostile media: he just kept telling us we were assholes, and every time he said it, he went up five points in the Gallup Poll.

Throughout his years in politics he sustained his contempt and occasionally took the trouble to give us a detailed account of his low opinion of this or that story or comment that had reached his attention. How it had reached him, as he supposedly never viewed or read, he didn't say.

Trudeau played the press conference game while shunning the scrums, especially after those confrontations became physical. But his promise of regular press conferences turned to dross when his long lectures and the paucity of news made them events to be avoided. I suspect he bored us deliberately, for he knew very well how to light up the newscasts when the devil moved him.

It was his belief, I think, that the press conference really has no place in the parliamentary system, except when a prime minister has something he wants to put over on the opposition. He found regular press conferences tedious, and he would often use them merely to enrage his opponents.

The one thing that Trudeau did achieve, or maybe others achieved it for him, was to ensure that media skepticism came to bear more heavily on his adversaries than on himself. Perhaps he cowed us. Even such a tiger as Vancouver's Jack Webster confessed that he turned to putty when Trudeau came on his show. Trudeau's domination of the media allowed him, among other things, to divert attention from the fact that Joe Clark consistently beat him in debate.

It was once the conventional wisdom that David Lewis was the only man in public life who could match wits and intellect with Trudeau, but neither man had enough respect for the other to comment on that.

Lewis detested Trudeau as an opportunist and pragmatist, as well he might, for Trudeau ditched his lifelong sympathy with the CCF/NDP and wound up three years later as Liberal prime minister of Canada.

Lewis also had an ingrained dislike for the rich, especially those who were born to it. For his part Trudeau looked down on Lewis and thought him overrated. Each man brought out the worst in the other, and the fact that the two came from opposite ends of Montreal may have had something to do with it.

Trudeau remains the only PM not to have had any cronies in the Press Gallery, when having them has always been a tradition with prime ministers, who find it handy to rely on trusted friends in the press corps to bring gossip and float trial balloons about policies in the making.

Trudeau had no friends in the media when he became prime minister, and he had none when he resigned. But that didn't prevent him from joking – or was he? – that he had always wanted to be a member of a press club.

He came in pronouncing us idiots, and he went out saying the same thing, and in the years between he enriched many of us by providing an abundance of news, views, outrages and achievements. All the while he remained unsure of anybody's name in the media horde, or "the scum" as he called it.

The upshot was that the accessibility that had marked the Diefenbaker and Pearson years was closed off. Trudeau converted Ottawa to a closed city, and he put fear into the hearts of once-forthcoming ministers and senior bureaucrats.

In the final analysis journalists found the man a disappointment, his promises of a new age, a new Camelot in Canada, unfulfilled.

Pearson once said in his own defence that the worst thing that could happen to this country would be a strong-minded prime minister. We almost had one in Pierre Trudeau, but he saved himself and us by abandoning his strong-mindedness in favor of pragmatism, correctly perceiving that that was the only way to hang onto office.

Thus minded, and blessed by weak opposition, he endured for sixteen years, though he was out of steam at the end and left his party utterly deflated and his country in debt up to its widely spaced ears.

"If I have committed any mistake," he once said, "it is in staying too close to absolute truths, rather than the conventional wisdom. A politician must take absolute truth and accommodate it to the facts around him."

Every prime minister has had that struggle, but only Trudeau had the nerve to say it out loud.

9. Clark

"There's no gain without pain."   – *Joe Clark*

If Robert Stanfield, as I once wrote, was "the best prime minister Canada never had," what does that make Joe Clark, who was better qualified for the work than Stanfield and who actually landed the job, only to be diddled out of it?

Better qualified because of his westernness at a time when the West was in the ascendancy. Better qualified because of his experience in the House of Commons, and his youth, and his bilingualism. Clark was trained for television and was able to get across in a twenty-second clip what it took Stanfield twenty minutes to say.

It is a safe assumption that Stanfield would have won the 1979 election had he stayed on as Tory leader. He then would have been prime minister for twenty years, minimum. It might have seemed like forty years, for they would have been dull years for those of us who thrive on political ferment. But instead,

Stanfield decided that three defeats at Trudeau's hands were enough, that he and the party could not afford the ten years required for his image to "take" as it had in Nova Scotia.

So the droopy-eyed man from Halifax gave way to a lop-eared kid from Rocky Mountain who had never held a job – apart from his seat in Parliament before he became national leader of the Progressive Conservative Party and faced the prospect of becoming prime minister.

Clark was the youngest man ever to reach that pinnacle, and he became the first western-born prime minister in history. (John Diefenbaker was born in Ontario, and R.B. Bennett was a New Brunswicker who made good in Calgary.)

The West had been clamoring for a place at the cabinet table. Trudeau had been reduced to using western senators as ministers. With Clark, westerners flocked at last to the inner councils of government.

But all at once it emerged that Joe Clark didn't seem to be a westerner at all. It wasn't just that he became preoccupied with his lack of seats in Quebec (like Trudeau, he used senators to fill in the cabinet blanks). Clark didn't talk like a westerner, he didn't walk like one, and he certainly didn't look like one – not if the western model is the lantern-jawed, leathery, range boss or the roughneck of the oil rig or the tractor driver in the wheat field. Nor was there anything of the Calgary boardroom about him, or the Edmonton bowling alley.

Could you picture Joe Clark on a horse? Or at the wheel of a pickup truck? Seeing is believing. His mother had a rusty half-ton truck she tooled around High River in, and one of the more memorable sights during Clark's prime ministership was the sight of Joe driving it when he was home, mom beside him, and the Mounties in their cars riding shotgun fore and aft, through the streets of what used to be the number one cowboy town in the West.

Joe Clark came to power without a majority, and his boldest and most fatal decision was to play it as John Diefenbaker had handled his minority in 1957. One year after his minority win, Diefenbaker swept the country. Clark's one-year-later saw him out of power and Pierre Trudeau back in.

All favorable parallels faded for Clark, and all the worst scenarios came into play in what his mate, Maureen McTeer, once described to me as "repeated journeys into hell."

Joe Clark was the only prime minister who treated reporters as his equals, or even as his superiors. It was unnerving to hear a prime minister call you sir when you were giving him the business.

This ill-conceived respect for reporters grew out of the high regard in which he held his journalist father and his father's colleagues. Joe had aspired to be a newspaperman himself, and in his biography he listed journalism as his profession, for lack of anything else.

But his greatest problem was always that he was such a ready target, his manners and mannerisms setting him up for that wimp label in spite of his cow-country background and his conquest of the French language, rare for an Albertan.

The wimping of Clark cost him his prime ministership and his party's leadership, and it was an unfair rap, from writers who built their own reputations by destroying Clark's.

The first, and worst, example was media coverage of Clark's round-the-world tour, four months before the 1979 election in which Clark won his short-lived minority mandate.

Without that hatchet job Clark might have won a majority, he might not have had to bear the subsequent defeat, the decline of his leadership and his replacement by Brian Mulroney.

He never did complain about the mangling he took on that tour from a horde of reporters who only signed on for the trip after polls told them he would be the next prime minister. Arrangements for the media crowd had to be made hastily on a variety of local and global airlines, and a lot of things went awry. Clark never got a fair shake from then on. The tour dispatches concentrated on what the leader of the pack, Allan

Fotheringham, called Clark's goofs, gaffes, fumbles and fiascos. Clark's reaction to the ridicule was, "That's up to you fellows."

Don Sellar of Southam News, taking his cue from Fotheringham, wrote that Clark's numerous "misspeaks," together with luggage problems, raised doubts about Clark's ability to be prime minister.

To his credit, Geoffrey Stevens of the *Globe and Mail* lamented "the churlishness of the accompanying journalists for whom no speck of lint is too small to pick."

And the *Toronto Sun* referred to the rat-pack syndrome: "Can't you just hear them over their evening drinks out – anecdoting one another with real and imagined Clark antics?"

"The people instinctively understand this syndrome," said the *Sun*, "and perhaps that's another reason why the media, generally, have too little respect these days."

But reporters continued to hang the labels on Clark, and to this day the popular impression is that he, personally, lost the laundry and luggage off Egypt Air in Bangkok; and that he alone embarrassed the Canadian press corps with a lack of knowledge of world affairs. Fotheringham had written off Clark as a fake during the tour: "clearly needs more international experience. . . ."

Dr. Foth, enhancing his own national standing, concluded that Clark and his entourage ended the tour "without their underwear or their reputations." In Jordan, Fotheringham gave top play to a yellow garbage truck that delayed the Clark convoy. And when Clark lost his footing while inspecting a military honor guard on the Golan Heights, Fotheringham wrote that "those of us watching almost demanded an instant slow-motion replay to confirm what our eyes had witnessed."

Southam's Sellar chimed in with: "Clark has turned in a personal performance that wavers between mediocre and pathetic."

Reporters on that trip have, through the years, defended their dispatches as being factual. When I chided Fotheringham for fattening himself at Clark's expense, he replied that if Clark was so fragile as to be vulnerable to his pen, then the guy wasn't up to much anyway.

"Somebody out there is trying to get me," Joe Clark told reporters back in 1979. To which I replied, "Mr. Prime Minister, *everybody* out here is trying to get you."

Joe Clark still speaks to the media people who did him in. But his mother doesn't.

His mother doesn't speak to any media people at all, as I discovered on a recent call at her home in High River to pay my respects. She was courteous but cautious, and she said she would kill me if I wrote about the visit. Nothing in particular transpired: I gave her the pie I'd bought at a local bake sale and marveled at the old Datsun pickup truck in her yard, which she told me was her favorite vehicle.

I left with the impression that she, like the rest of us, expects to see and hear a great deal more of her political offspring. Perhaps, notwithstanding all the past bad press, another go as PM isn't out of reach for this hardworking, serious but open-hearted man.

Joe Clark's warmest act toward me came in 1981. Claudy Mailly and I had just set up housekeeping in circumstances that scandalized both our circles, and we felt ostracized – unwanted anywhere.

But when we showed up at Joe and Maureen's garden party at Stornoway, they both gave us a friendly greeting. In a loud voice Joe said, "You will always be welcome in our house."

The result was not exactly re-entry into the social whirl, yet it was something neither of us will forget. Sure, they could hardly have thrown us out, but their kindness was beyond anything we might have expected – and the strawberries and champagne were terrific!

Whenever Joe Clark showed warmth, as he often did and does, it was never with the sheen that so many politicians develop to deal with masses of people. Clark conveys the feeling that he knows whom he's talking to and is genuinely interested. Insincerity is not part of his makeup. I can't imagine him doing anything dishonest, let alone rotten or callous.

When his leadership was being challenged and dirty tricks were being played, especially in Quebec, Clark pursed his lips and told his followers to "do what you have to do, but don't tell me about it." When the dust settled, those handlers – and Clark – went to work for Brian Mulroney in the cause of party unity.

In spite of the clobbering he took from the media, he never attacked his detractors head on. He was unfailingly courteous to questions, however hostile, and was more forthcoming than any prime minister before or since. To him, the Trudeau technique of the putdown, either to the public or journalists, was unknown.

Under stress he ate junk food and steaks like old boots. He drank Coke by the gallon, switching to chocolate milk shakes when the stress was most severe. He gave no thought to gourmet food, or even for the hearty, healthy fare his mother and Maureen tried to force upon him. In this he resembled John Diefenbaker, who in his darkest moments would gobble ice cream.

Clark is the only prime minister who ever asked me for advice. He used to do that with journalists, whenever he got together with them one on one. And it wasn't a sneering session, the way it was with Trudeau the few times we met him privately.

My advice to Clark was the same he received from every quarter: "You've got to do something about Quebec."

He smiled. "I know. I'm trying."

So he was. So had Stanfield, and Clark was better at the lingo than old Big Thunder was. As a matter of fact Clark was better at French than almost any anglo, certainly any western one. But it didn't make any difference in Quebec. He toured the province, he gave interviews, he went on hot lines, he made speeches, he drew applause, he never messed up. And still the French wouldn't vote for him, and that finished him, as prime minister and party leader, setting the stage for Trudeau's last stand and ensuring the Mulroney succession.

The voters did themselves a disservice. In Clark they had a politician who took the wishes of the people on the street into account. During his successful 1979 campaign he promised to restore the supremacy of Parliament by encouraging Tory MPs to speak out when they disagreed with government policy. "After all," he told the crowd, "these men and women are your MPs, not my MPs."

It would be hard to imagine Pierre Trudeau, much less John Diefenbaker, saying that. Dief, who had opposed Clark's bid for the party leadership and who ridiculed him once he got the job, called Clark's election as prime minister "a black day in Canada's history." There were many who agreed with the old Chief's appraisal, but in the light of all that has happened since, it wasn't one of his better judgments.

Diefenbaker's opponent had been Pearson – never a hot item with voters – advised by Jack Pickersgill, who had been in high places so long his judgment was fogged and who had turned into a leprechaun in his role as the adopted son of Bonavista-Twillingate.

Clark's opponent was Trudeau – reluctant but ready for one more kick at the can – advised by the wily Allan MacEachen, the pudgy Cape Breton recluse with the snapping eyes and the fighting instincts of a mongoose.

It was no contest. Clark's undoing was MacEachen's masterpiece.

MacEachen had a lot of help. Help from Tories unsure of Clark, and help from a media that treated Clark as a joke that rollicked the nation and had Albertans laughing harder than anybody.

In fact, Clark was no wimp, then or now. The problem was how to counter the constant dosages of image poison, short of body building. There were lessons in how to walk more purposefully and how to swing the arms and work the hands less convulsively. Hairdressers were brought in from Toronto to mitigate the shape of his head and make his ears seem higher.

These things took center stage in the media, and the true qualities of the man, evident to all who dealt with him at close quarters, never did get through. He was smarter, better humored, better informed, and more gutsy than the Canadian public ever knew while he was prime minister.

He handled himself well in the House of Commons, besting Trudeau in debate on the few occasions Trudeau deigned to face him in either government or later opposition. That in itself is not so remarkable – Stanfield won every Commons debate he ever had with Trudeau – but Clark also handled TV as Stanfield never could and as Trudeau seldom bothered to do. Clark snapped off the TV clips by instinct, and yet all that people noticed were his receding chin and his shiny complexion.

From the opposition benches in the Commons he had towered over the NDP's Ed Broadbent. But by disparaging Broadbent, he ensured the later opposition of the New Democrats to his government, despite his leftward leanings. The NDP held the balance of power and used it on their first serious confidence vote to bring Joe Clark down, thus ensuring Trudeau's return in the subsequent election.

Why Broadbent wanted to do that has never been satisfactorily explained, apart from the routine anti-budget mouthings and his lame claim that he wanted to be prime minister. More likely the answer lies in Broadbent's hatred of the Tories, and the evidence that the NDP would never support a Tory minority government, however uncomfortable they might be with a Liberal one.

Why the Liberals wanted to bring Clark down is almost as puzzling, if you discount the Grit hunger for power at any price. At the time, many Liberals felt that their party needed a rebuilding spell out of office after the long Pearson-Trudeau years; they were content to let the Tories take the rap for a predicted economic recession and for a needed assault on the deficit. Instead, the Trudeau Liberals ended up bearing the brunt of hard times.

As prime minister, Clark was driven up the wall by the mere mention of William Davis, the Conservative premier of Ontario, and Davis's political apparatus, known as "the Big Blue Machine." The feeling was mutual; Davis had as little time for Joe Clark as Pierre had. During the fight over oil prices – Davis wanted down, Lougheed wanted up, and Clark was on Lougheed's side, advocating the world price – telephone conversations between Clark and Davis were cold-war icy.

In the end Davis contributed to Clark's election defeat and loss of the party leadership. But in one respect, at least, Joe Clark had the last laugh. His example as a bilingual prime minister meant that after him no unilingual anglo could aspire to be prime minister of Canada (no unilingual franco had *ever* been able to.) This killed any ambitions Davis might have had for the brass ring. Peter Lougheed, who had belittled Clark almost as much as Davis had, paid the same price and had to abandon his prime-ministerial dream.

The night they put Pierre Trudeau back in power, Clark barely controlled his rage. There was humiliation and the foreknowledge of recriminations in Tory ranks, but mainly there was anger: "Those arrogant SOBs are going to be simply impossible in the Commons!" And when his mother tried to comfort him by mussing his hair, he shook her off. It had been a rotten campaign, and the next three years would be even worse. At one stage in his losing struggle Clark was reduced to making a speech about the potential of the potato as a power source; the Chamber of Commerce in Summerside, Prince Edward Island, had decreed no politics in his speech, so the poor guy had to talk about potatoes.

The courage of the man should have made a mockery of the "wimp" charges. During the final years of his leadership, that courage was there for all to see. But overshadowing it, in the public eye, was his apparent lack of style.

He hasn't got a trendy bone in his body, and it was inevitable that he would be compared unfavorably to more stylish MPs, particularly to Pierre Trudeau (a fate that befell most politicians who crossed Pierre's path).

The irony is that Clark was more in tune with the times than Trudeau on many of the questions of the day. On women's rights Clark was miles ahead, not only of Trudeau but of most Canadians. And he flared if it was suggested that this was simply Maureen McTeer's influence. "I believe in it," he once growled at my wife, Claudy, when she lauded McTeer's feminist influence on him.

On ecological questions, on provincial rights, and on the need to humanize politics, Clark was progressive enough to merit the tag of Red Tory. He also sought to reform the system of patronage; in fact he delayed so long in making his appointments (because of the meticulous searches he ordered to ensure the best candidates for public jobs) that he was out of office before he could act.

Once, when Claudy brought word back from her old boss, Earle McLaughlin, chairman of the Royal Bank, about how the country should be run, Clark said angrily: "Tell McLaughlin that no advice is needed from a man who dishes out all that baloney about how he can't find a woman qualified to sit on his board of directors!"

In his leanings toward the Third World, he matches Mulroney's own concerns and brings at least as much punch to Canada's image as Trudeau's showboating ever did. When his criticism of Israeli abuses of Palestinian refugees and his criticism of Sikh terrorists collided with the Jewish and Sikh communities in Canada, he stood his ground even while admitting he had underestimated the depths of the disapproval aimed at him. In both cases he carried majority Canadian opinion with him - and majority world opinion, as well, including the support of many Jews and Sikhs.

His chosen field in the Mulroney cabinet being the very arena where his earlier critics dubbed him a booby, he has demonstrated his worth and abilities as he never had while prime minister. He became in the view of many, including Mulroney, our most effective foreign minister since Lester Pearson.

Now we know that Joe Clark is nimble-minded, shrewd, courteous to his advisers and at ease in extensive travels. He enters political mine fields without fear, angering Jews, Sikhs and others in the process but still holding firm while his boss tries to placate the protesters. Through it all Clark uses his parliamentary smarts to help the Mulroney team, particularly on days when it falls to him to be acting prime minister during Question Period.

In a cabinet wracked by scandals and incompetence in its opening years, Clark was a rock, inside and outside the House of Commons. He and Mulroney became an effective team, a credit to both men: Mulroney the unifier, Clark the loyal lieutenant and party servant.

The Joe Clark of today is a much wiser man than he was as prime minister. Not being PM obviously contributes to wisdom.

Two things strike most people when they meet Clark.

One is that he is much taller than they expect. During Trudeau's time Clark had seemed small, when in fact he towered over Pierre.

The other thing is Clark's sense of humor.

When Claudy first ran as a Tory candidate in Montreal, she met Clark to submit her credentials and to look over the leader about whom Quebeckers knew so little.

The litany of her qualifications was recited for Clark's benefit: bilingual, an economist, a business woman, a mother, an author, a Quebec nationalist, a world traveller, a fighter for women's rights and an advocate of the poor, having grown up in Montreal's east end. Also, an ethnic, through her Polish-Canadian mother.

Clark laughed. Not the "ho, ho, ho" of his mimics, but a relaxed belly laugh. "Were you born in a manger?" he asked.

"No," she answered. "On a table in an Iberville Street kitchen."

"That's what I like in a candidate," chuckled Clark. "Modesty."

Claudy ran against André Ouellet in the Montreal riding of Papineau and got creamed. Then, after serving as press secretary to Clark and subsequently to Mulroney, she made it in Gatineau as part of the Mulroney Quebec avalanche.

But always there is a place in her heart for the man we in media called "Little Joe" – who may not be so little after all.

10. Meighen to Mulroney

"This is no time for mellow men."   – *John Turner*

Arthur Meighen wanted to save the Empire, and failed.

Meighen had two brief kicks at the prime ministerial can, and missed because of King's machinations. If Meighen is remembered at all, it is for defending railroad robber barons, for the Conscription Bill in 1917, and for his too rigid loyalty to Britain.

Meighen was the epitome of all that Quebeckers found distasteful in the Conservative Party, and he did more than anything except the hanging of Louis Riel to keep the party unpopular in Quebec.

Nevertheless, we have the word of Grattan O'Leary and Fulgence Carpentier that Meighen was the idol of most reporters of his day. I saw him just once, in 1958. He came (by mistake – he thought he would be listening to the eloquent and erudite Max Freedman) to hear a speech I was giving at the

Empire Club in Toronto. His icy edge would melt on occasions such as the Press Gallery dinner. (Maybe he felt secure that he was fulfilling tradition, as that irreverent bunfest, begun in 1867, was and is the oldest fraternal evening in the land.)

His way with quotations in his speeches was much admired. The story goes that on a return voyage from Australia he received a cabled invitation to speak on Shakespeare in Vancouver. As there was no volume of Shakespeare on the ship, Meighen prepared his talk from his own profound knowledge of the bard, and his lengthy quotations were word perfect.

R. B. Bennett was the fourth Canadian prime minister from the Maritimes, a region that once shared with the old Dominion of Virginia the title of "mother of leaders." Like Virginia, the Maritimes faded in national importance, and the odds are that Bennett will be the last PM from that part of our country.

Most people thought Bennett was an Albertan. He came from the New Brunswick strain that produced Wacky Bennett and Son of British Columbia, and my family's feeling about his people (we had several of them as neighbors and friends) was that they were better suited to wild western politics than to eastern.

R.B. Bennett never cared a hoot about his native province, and when the voters brought his political career to an end, he wiped his feet of Canada altogether and took off for Britain. There he lived out his remaining years in the countryside next door to old friend, protégé and fellow New Brunswicker Lord Beaverbrook, who engineered a viscountcy for him.

And there he died, in a scalding tub of water that was kept boiling by a gas geyser until he was found in the morning. That he was parboiled did not emerge until a servant divulged it years later.

Bennett's memory lives on chiefly because of the Bennett Library named for him at Beaverbrook's beloved University of

New Brunswick in Fredericton, one of many Beaverbrook projects on that hilltop campus. In my later meetings with him, Beaverbrook maintained that Bennett was the most brilliant politician he had ever known.

Mackenzie King was born old. He seemed old when I first saw him in Vancouver in the 1940 campaign; much older when I next saw him at the Quebec Conference with Churchill and Roosevelt in 1943; and very old in his last year in office, when I came to Ottawa in 1947.

Although he was renowned for his dullness, I knew of otherwise sober and sane men who swore to kill him, who used his name as a cuss word. For along with his political skill he possessed the selfish meanness not unusual in political leaders.

Physically, King was the least prepossessing of our prime ministers – short, squat, waddly when he walked, bald of pate but with great tufts of hair growing out of his overlarge ears.

His wardrobe was meager, and he wore his suits until they were threadbare. It is said that his chauffeur-valet quit his employ upon finding that King's long underwear consisted more of the valet's darning than of the original material.

Since none of us in the press corps ever enjoyed King's hospitality, we had no first-hand experience of his stinginess. But there were clues.

A favorite aunt of mine lived in a log house on King's preferred route to his estate at Kingsmere, and King dropped in on her from time to time for a cup of tea and some cake. He urged her to open a roadside tearoom, and she took the idea seriously before realizing that what he really wanted was a place along the way where he could eat and sip for free.

It was also no secret that he paid slave wages and made his employees earn every penny. The stone walls at Kingsmere, which form a framework for today's tourist trails, were built by one man who labored for years for a miserable thirty dollars a month, plus room and board. King's aides worked endless hours under wretched conditions; they wondered if there was any compassion in the man at all.

A lifelong bachelor, King may also have been a womanizer. His voluminous diaries are ambiguous on this point – we can't be sure whether he dallied with Ottawa's marketplace whores in hopes of reforming them or of helping them turn a trick. In his diaries as well were revelations about his spiritualism, his obsessions, his phobias and his dreams.

He was not typical in any way. At a time when draft dodging was rare, he avoided involvement in the First World War by going to the United States. Nonetheless he won the 1940 election over a strongly militaristic opponent and ran the government very well indeed during the intense mobilization that gave Canada global military stature.

He did it without "image," without public relations or press officers, without interviews or press conferences, without a semblance of charisma. In an age when speeches were the stuff of politics, within Parliament and without, he was the most boring speaker imaginable.

Over members of his cabinet, on the other hand, he had a hold unmatched by any prime minister. And the members of his cabinet were no slouches. It was said at the time that the nation had never seen their like before, and many believe that their like has never been seen since.

But as a politician King will mostly be remembered for his procrastination, compromising, scheming and trickery. The problems he postponed facing, in particular the French-English one, came back to haunt his successors.

He had no sense of the regions or their ambitions. He hastened the breaking of the British tie without knowing what to put in its place, and as a consequence the cultural and economic Americanization of Canada spread like wildfire during the 1930s and 1940s.

Behind his back every politician and member of the press

called him "Willie," but to his face everyone called him Mr. King. Long after he was gone, people continued to speak of him that way.

It was taken for granted throughout his tenure that he was not available to the press. With rare exceptions, such as his cultivation of reporter Grant Dexter as a contact with the editor of the *Winnipeg Free Press* (then of international stature as a liberal organ), he had no need of us, nor we of him. The debates in the Commons had to provide the running story, and God knows he contributed endlessly to those.

Cocktail parties were just coming into fashion in 1947. It was not King's custom to attend them; but he did show up at one or two such functions staged by the Press Gallery. In fact, it was after a lot of imbibing of mixed drinks by the assembled press, at the end of the annual Press Gallery dinner, that King announced his intention to retire. This was a bit of mischief on his part. Not only did we have to get his permission to suspend the off-the-record rule so that the news could be reported to the nation, but when we did report it, we were all in an advanced state of inebriation.

The Prime Minister enjoyed his prank enormously.

King's successor, Louis St. Laurent, was an old-world gentleman when the breed was fading fast but not yet extinct. The manners of this aging ex-lawyer were reflected in the style of his clothes: the morning coat, the striped trousers, the hard collars, the neat foulard cravats and, in the winter, the velvet-collared overcoats.

I don't recall my first meeting with "the old man," as we came to call him. I only remember becoming aware of his presence as a potent member of Mackenzie King's last cabinet and then as King's own favorite for the succession, though St. Laurent was King's junior by just six years.

He was sixty-six when he became PM. It was not an easy succession, partly because St. Laurent's stiffness was thought to be a handicap and partly because the principle of English-French alternation of PMs (or "dat damn alternance," as Jean Chrétien would one day curse it) was not yet widely accepted. But aide Jack Pickersgill kept telling us it was going to be all right.

We already knew that postwar times were good and that St. Laurent's Tory opponent, George Drew, was a stuffed shirt from Toronto. What we did not suspect was that St. Laurent would govern for nine years that would be looked back on as the most serene in the nation's history. The reassuring figure of Louis St. Laurent fit in perfectly, despite the fact that many of his fellow Quebeckers thought of him as a sellout and most English-speaking Canadians didn't think of him at all.

His bilingualism was taken as a given. Weren't all French Canadians supposed to be bilingual? Of his perfect mastery of both languages he said that, when he was growing up, he assumed that all children spoke English to their mothers and French to their fathers.

He lacked the cunning of King, the rascality and roguishness of Duplessis (who could mimic St. Laurent perfectly as a relic of ages past) or the rudeness of C.D. Howe. Yet in a time when petty corruption was still rife in Canadian elections, with the Quebec Liberals playing the game as flagrantly as Duplessis himself, it was impossible to imagine St. Laurent soiling his perfectly manicured hands.

Even after the pipeline scandal brought his government down, and he was groggy to the point of exhaustion, the man still seemed to be above the battle, though all was lost. I think he would have made a marvelous cardinal – or even pope (although his occasional outbursts of temper might go over badly at the modern Vatican).

St. Laurent's times were the times of Harry Truman and Dwight Eisenhower in the United States, and the country he led was absorbing the same changes in electronic reporting and mass media that were so radically transforming society to the south of us and would complicate the lives of every subsequent Canadian prime minister.

You have seen what it did to Diefenbaker, Pearson, Trudeau, and Clark. But the biggest mess-up was John Turner.

Turner's honeymoon with the media lasted for eight years – while he was on sabbatical from politics. He was lionized as the prime-minister-in-waiting and listed at the top of every media mention of Trudeau's successor.

It was a long press build-up, and it kept John Turner's name and fame alive. It fueled his leadership campaign when Trudeau resigned, and it carried him to his leadership win over Jean Chrétien, the deserving candidate of whom party president Iona Campagnolo said, "He is second in our votes but first in our hearts."

The minute Turner triumphed, it was Chrétien whom the Liberals, the people – and the media – suddenly realized they loved. Having invented John Turner as Trudeau's successor and potential prime minister, the media now pronounced him rusty and out of date and helped make a farce of an election campaign that he entered as a winner and emerged from as one of Canadian history's biggest losers.

For Turner this media turnabout was the second piece of bad luck in an otherwise charmed life. The first was Trudeau's refusal to retire ten years earlier, when Turner was hot. That disappointment drove Turner into the depths of Toronto, where he fattened his bank account while his political skills were dulled by the martinis at Winston's and flattery in the boardrooms and bistros.

Had Turner lost his Vancouver seat in the 1984 Tory landslide, it would have been the end of him politically. As it was, he survived to face a Liberal Party in ferment and to provide the media with a long-running sideshow to its new main event: the life and times of Mulroney.

John Turner thought he had a camaraderie with media.

Indeed he had, when he quit the Trudeau cabinet. But when he returned after his golden years on Bay Street, most of his old pals were gone. In the Parliamentary Press Gallery there is an annual turnover in membership of at least one-third, the average age being somewhere in the low thirties, so there are always new young faces in the national press corps to take the older politicians by surprise and trip them up.

Also, when Turner came back, a greatly increased number of reporters were women – tougher, more skeptical, more militant, better informed than any group of reporters before them. Despite Turner's desperate efforts to shake the locker-room image and jocktalk, he plummeted from the top of the polls to the bottom in record time, with the media speeding his fall and kicking away the safety net.

He never did face the House of Commons as prime minister. Thus he was at least spared the torment of Question Period and the gnashing and grinding of the scrums. Yet in light of his campaign performance, he probably wished he *had* met Parliament and been given a chance to smooth out some of the kinks there before taking the country to the polls.

His equilibrium has yet to be restored. Maybe he should write a book. Jean Chrétien created a sensation with his book, *Straight From the Heart*, a critical and commercial success throughout the land, which confirmed him as one of Canada's best-loved politicians. Would anybody buy a Turner book?

Who is Canada's best-dressed politician? Brian Mulroney.

In fact, he's officially one of Canada's best-dressed men. And don't think Brian didn't enjoy being on that list as much as anything that has happened to him in politics. He's always hoped that someday the media brigade would say he got something right.

Nobody ever questioned Pierre Trudeau's mandate to run the country, but Mulroney's opponents question his credentials all the time, although he fashioned the biggest majority ever in the House of Commons.

On issue after issue, spokesmen for the Liberals and New Democrats have said that Mulroney lost the right to implement his policies on everything from free trade with the U.S. to the staffing of his own office. Their argument was that since a series of scandals put the government at the bottom of the opinion polls, it no longer had the right to act in the name of the people of Canada.

This rubbish caught on. But the idea that a government cannot make decisions unless it has evident voter support on every issue has no historical justification. Many of our past leaders' boldest initiatives were never part of their election campaigns. Diefenbaker canceled the Avro Arrow without going to the people. Pearson gave us our flag without putting the matter to public vote. Trudeau patriated the constitution and put in the Charter of Rights and Freedoms without any sort of referendum.

Medicare, unemployment insurance, the Canada Pension Plan, family allowances – all were brought in by governments without specific endorsement from the voters. Canada entered two world wars and the Korean conflict without checking with voters. Similarly, our peacekeeping efforts in the Middle East and elsewhere were unendorsed by election or referendum.

But Brian does not deserve to lead, went the cry.

And so his government kept losing momentum. It was described as wallowing in a sea of scandal, except that none of the scandals had any criminal content and most would have been the stuff of comedy in more forgiving times, or in countries with real problems. When there were no new scandals, media rehashed the old ones.

Mulroney has delivered good results all along the line. He displays two qualities seldom found in one person: total confidence in his own judgment and the ability to laugh at himself. These strengths have helped him fulfill virtually all his main promises on the economy, the constitution and relations with the United States. Mulroney's times were tranquil for Canadians (however unsettling they may have been for Tories).

His dealings with the provincial governments were conducted, as pledged, in tones of civility – for the first time in half a century.

And yet the man got no credit. Worse, he was regarded with suspicion and called Myron Baloney and Ryan Babooney and even Lyin' Brian, sometimes to his face.

Because he tends to overstate the case either for or against his own government, he has the reputation of bending the truth. And his syrupy vocal tones, so low they seem to be coming from his boots, make him sound oily. His voice can be very effective when it's in a higher register and he's speaking spontaneously, but at such times he's liable to get carried away and say things his advisers wish he wouldn't.

What's a best-dressed man to do?

One of his biggest mistakes was to hire as aides most of the reporters and columnists who were favorable to him, notably L. Ian MacDonald, Bruce Phillips, Dalton Camp, Michel Gratton, and Bill Fox. With them effectively silenced, the media field was left largely to the carpers, doubters and exposers.

Mulroney's opening scrum as PM was marked by his crying out, when jostled by the media mob: "Hey, lookit, we're all friends here!"

The mob let out a groan – how could any prime minister entertain such a naive thought?

(Always in Mulroney's conversations is the word "lookit." It's what he punches home his sentences with. It's a word from the streets and locker rooms and can stand for, "Lemme tellya," or "Ya better believe it," or Trudeau's "Listen, Buster," or, what Mulroney uses it most of the time to mean, "Ya dance with the one that brung ya.")

Mulroney used to be a great media junkie. For most of his adult life he loved the company of newspaper people, and he sailed into office on a wave of media support. But he underestimated the degree to which this support was the working press's revenge on Trudeau.

"We'll give 'em style," he said, and so he did, in his fashion. His parties for the media were famous for having the best food, the best drinks, the best times, year after year.

But even this rebounded on him, when the press became more interested in the price tag than the party. Before long he had become the one world leader whose diplomatic travels were written about in terms of their expense rather than their accomplishments.

The roster of Mulroney's ministers involved in questionable activities started to sound like a gang-up on Quebec by the anglo press (at least, that's how a number of writers in Quebec saw it). Marcel Masse and his election expenses, Suzanne Blais-Grenier and her limousines, André Bissonnette and the land flip, Roch LaSalle and the peddling of favors, Michel Côté and his undisclosed loan. . . . Finally, in desperation, Mulroney brought in Lucien Bouchard as "Mr. Clean," and was accused of buying votes.

Mulroney himself regards the "scandals" as trivia and says, "Conflict of interest was dormant throughout all of Trudeau's mandate. Just look at the conflicts of interest that would drive a minister or a prime minister from office today that were commonplace in his regime."

What the government's adversaries were asking behind all this mud-slinging was whether Mulroney was part of the clean new politics of Quebec, epitomized by René Lévesque, or the dirty old politics of Maurice Duplessis.

Mulroney seemed no more fortunate in his choices of Quebec ministers than was an earlier Tory PM, John Diefenbaker. (The only prime minister who ever had strong Quebec ministers was Pierre Trudeau.) But however much Mulroney might like to trade his Quebec contingent for the likes of Jean Chrétien or Marc Lalonde or Jean-Luc Pepin or Monique Bégin, the deficiencies of his party's French connection did not make him a crook, nor should they contribute to what his critics keep calling Mulroney's "sleaze factor." Trudeau had sixteen years in which to earn his good marks for cabinet appointments, and most of those marks were earned in mid-term.

Mulroney's present cabinet is, without question, too big. His excuse is that he was a prisoner of an enormous majority. He appointed thirty MPs to be parliamentary secretaries to forty ministers and then cloaked additional MPs with extra pay and responsibility as committee chairmen. John Diefenbaker's 1957 cabinet comprised seventeen ministers with twelve parliamentary secretaries; his 1958 cabinet, after the landslide victory, had twenty-three ministers.

The big thing Mulroney did right was to bring Joe Clark and all Clark's supporters on board in positions of responsibility. Thus reunited, the Tory party has stayed united through bad luck, incompetence, corruption and inexperience - through some of the roughest years any majority government has ever suffered.

It is to Mulroney's credit that other old opponents served him so well: John Crosbie, Michael Wilson, Flora MacDonald, and Don Mazankowski. Helping the Tory cause was the ineptitude of the Liberal opposition. That, and the fact that the Conservatives had time to get the hang of governing and came to employ advisers who seemed to know something about the business.

But the Tories' greatest advantage - and the one presumed so often to be their greatest liability - is Mulroney himself. More than for any PM before him, his job is beyond human ability to perform capably. The obstacles to performance now greatly exceed the powers available. And yet, misdeeds and all, Mulroney kept trying, even succeeding, as he did with flying colors at the Toronto Economic Summit.

For a take-home pay of about $142,000 plus expenses, he was supposed to deliver unbounded managerial and leadership skills, in devoted service to the nation and for the betterment of the people.

His skill with our two maternal languages is exceptional - he is not only bilingual but bicultural. When he speaks French, he becomes French. (He is the only person of my acquaintance who can be completely Irish in French.) He is living, walking, talking proof that bilingualism works and that a person can bridge the two solitudes and be accepted in both.

And he has preserved his sense of humor. It is one of the principal sources of his charm in both its anglo and franco modes. It keeps him sane, as does his cussing, which he does casually and in genuine anger or anguish (and always off the record). There is a spontaneity to him that has survived the usual dehumanizing of the PM. Put him next to a piano and he's singing his heart out, devil take the advisers who keep telling him to stop.

He remains ever optimistic. To my mind, he was at his best in his speech of October 1987:

"We go forward with confidence in our future, confidence in our country, and most of all, confidence in the youth of Canada. We have set a course for a stronger, a more united, and a more prosperous Canada. It is not a path – it never was and never will be – for the faint of heart, but this country was not built by timid souls. This is a path for the daring, the innovative, and the nation-builders who are now called upon to make a firm decision on behalf of a strong, united and prosperous Canada."

Mulroney says he doesn't mind any longer when the media razzes him for words like those – "I learned not to pay attention about two years ago, after I got kicked around a couple of years."

He also doesn't buy the bit about the job being impossible – "there will always be enough people after it."

Why?

"Because at the end of the day if you do your job right you can do an enormous amount. Lookit – I'll lay our first four years against the first four years of any prime minister in modern times. Not sixteen years. Just four years."

How does he keep sane despite the difficulties?

Difficulties? "You mean challenges!"

11. Here and There

"Metric will put us on a par with the United States, which will soon follow in our footsteps."   – *Jean-Luc Pepin, 1970*

From the moment leaders become prime minister, they are no longer people.

They brandish their tickets on the Titanic and soon subside into a life without friends or respect for having taken on such a rotten job (though nobody made them do it, and there are plenty of others to take their place).

And yet the prime minister has to give the appearance of normalcy. His public persona must combine a leader's ability to say the right things in public and to understand his and the country's place in the world with the average guy's interest in sports and making money and having a regular job to fall back on.

That's a tall order, and some PMs have filled it better than others.

None of them has been athletes in their spare time. But they have all tended to be healthy compared to their American counterparts. Or perhaps it's a case of not being shot at.

Apart from Trudeau, who went in for high diving, skiing, jogging, karate and yoga, the principal sports of prime ministers have been fishing and golf.

St. Laurent golfed. Diefenbaker fished. Pearson fished and golfed. Mulroney sponsored fishing parties, treating fishing as a backdrop for scheming and plotting politics.

Actually, fishing is a good cover for whatever game is afoot, and we've been assured that St. Peter doesn't count fishing days as part of one's allotted span on earth.

There was a time when it just seemed like good politics to be seen holding up a fish. This was before Greenpeace gave blood sports a bad name. It was also before expense accounts became the stuff of scandal in high places, although Diefenbaker did get into a bit of a jam when it was suggested that one Yukon trip – netting one fish – had cost $10,000.

Pearson, whose favorite sport was baseball, only fished to lighten up his image. Unlike a real fisherman, he never boasted about his catches or about the ones that got away. He had a four-mile lake as his private preserve in the Gatineaus but dismissed it as indifferent fishing water. Generations of natives who had poached the place would have disagreed.

Diefenbaker had a higher opinion of the lake's yield and shared its bounty with guests, including President Dwight D. Eisenhower.

Diefenbaker took vast hauls out of Lac la Ronge in northern Saskatchewan. It was in that rugged country that he also honed his skills as an avid hunter. But there weren't any votes in hunting, so Diefenbaker accentuated the angling, wearing out a whole generation of young media people trying to keep pace with him on his expeditions.

My admiration of Diefenbaker as a true angler was clinched one day in Glacier National Park, Montana, where the local state governor put the PM onto a pond that had been stocked with trout. Diefenbaker made a few casts, to no avail.

A park ranger standing beside him hooked a beauty, reeled it halfway in, and handed the rod to our man. Dief cranked in the fish. But when photographers invited him to hold it up, he declined: it was not his catch.

Pearson once had his picture taken with a fine salmon by the banks of the Restigouche; and we had to believe it was his fish, as he was an honorable man.

Trudeau couldn't stand fishing: the very thought of the hook gave him the creeps. His father owned a piece of Blue Bonnet raceway, but Pierre didn't take to the sport of kings, either.

Nor did he like football. The Grey Cup game on November 30, 1969, was played in the Montreal Autostade, on the Expo site. It was the coldest game day ever. Prime Minister Trudeau wore a crocheted ensemble that was described as a gift. For the official kick-off he donned cleated boots, though the players were wearing broomball shoes on the frozen turf. His kick set a record for awfulness.

His garb at the game evoked as much comment as the kilt he wore to a Scottish ball in Montreal the week before. The kilt was also a gift, from the Liberal caucus, and Pierre completed the outfit himself with belt, sporran and skean dhu. Fashion critics said he cut a brave figure, but one Highlander, referring to Trudeau's mother's side of the family, grumbled: "The Elliotts were border people who scorned the kilt."

Trudeau once revealed that he had wanted to be a ballet dancer, and his pirouettes certainly became famous. He even retired from the PM's job with a pirouette on stage to the tune of Paul Anka's "My Way." Even in mimicry he twirled with grace.

Of the prime ministers still with us, only Joe Clark is entirely unathletic. Turner is tennis. And Mulroney, though not especially sporty, has overcome his drinking and smoking and keeps himself commendably trim, fighting a problem with his sense of balance accentuated by vertigo.

Canada is a nation that lives on sport, as a glance at our newspapers and weekend TV will confirm. But the office of prime minister has not put its stamp on sports competition in the same way that, for example, the Governor-General's Awards recognize artistic endeavor. (Nobody considers the Pearson Cup a mug of much baseball prestige.)

Some politicians other than prime ministers have been excellent sportsmen. Don Getty quarterbacked the Edmonton Eskimos; Peter Lougheed, whom Getty succeeded as Alberta's premier, was punt return man for that team. Wags contend that both men were left groggy from too many tackles.

A couple of hockey stars became MPs, but didn't shine. Figure skater Otto Jelinek, however, became a cabinet minister, as did one-time speed skater Flora MacDonald. Canada's athlete of the century, Lionel Conacher, made it as an MP but dropped dead running out a hit on The Hill during a softball game against the Press Gallery.

Another leisure activity prime ministers have been known to indulge in, without great success, is writing – about themselves.

Mackenzie King produced copious diaries and in them rarely admitted to a mistake in his political career.

Lester Pearson's book about his term in office was written to set the record straight but did no more more to improve the art of political biography than Diefenbaker's ghost-written volumes. Both Pearson and Diefenbaker wrote marvellous first volumes, but these were yarns about their early years and had nothing to do with politicking or prime ministering.

Mulroney's *Where I Stand* did the job and nothing more, being a collection of speeches written by flacks.

Every publisher in Canada wants to get a memoir out of Pierre Trudeau. If one succeeds, you can bet that, like Mackenzie King, Trudeau will acknowledge no fault and the book will be heavy going, however well it sells.

More ministers quit Trudeau's cabinet than left Mulroney's, but Trudeau handled these departures simply: he never mentioned the ministers' names again. I doubt that a memoir would, either.

Trudeau was never a warm-hearted writer. His introduction to his 1963 translation of his collection of essays about Quebec's asbestos strike, published when he was still a so-called journalist, remains a brilliant summary of the Quebec of the time but is totally lacking a human touch.

Despite the overall mediocrity of our prime ministers' writing, nothing will stop the flood of books about the country's top job and the men who do it. Read on.

Books about media proliferate alongside books about politics. Media people do books on both media and politics. No politician has yet done a book about media, although not for a shortage of things to say. And it may happen yet.

Joe Clark's prime ministership was destroyed by the things others wrote about him. Maureen McTeer is avenging him. Her first salvo is a book for eighth graders, called *Parliament*. It outlines every aspect of the institution but doesn't once mention the Parliamentary Press Gallery.

I took her to task about this. She got that gleam in her eye and said that nobody in the Press Gallery was elected.

In vain did I argue with her that many people in and around Parliament are not elected, yet hold honored positions; for naught did I point out that Parliament must have had a purpose in conceding a newsroom and lounge for the media and furnishing credentials that entitle the holders to move freely about the buildings, eat in the restaurants, read in the libraries and park cars on the pavements.

She would have none of it, although she has dabbled in print and electronic media. Maybe she was hoping to shape a new generation of voters who will ignore the media and heed the voices of the politicians.

Some hope. The speeches of most of our prime ministers only put us to sleep. Prime-ministerial speeches are all self-justification, with little insight and less humor.

King and St. Laurent had confidence in their own judgment but lacked the ability to laugh at themselves. Pearson could laugh at himself but lacked confidence in his own judgment. Trudeau exuded confidence but never laughed at himself in his life. Clark had the laughter, but not the confidence. Turner had neither.

I have often felt that the general absence of humor in high places comes from the fact that so many of our prime ministers have been lawyers. Studying or practising law is part of their path to public success and private wealth.

Neither King nor Pearson were men of law, but each had a narrow escape.

At the turn of the century King's father taught law at Osgoode Hall in Toronto and encouraged his son to study the subject. King did look at law, along with political science, economics and constitutional history for an honors BA in 1895. After that he did spare-time studying of law while working as a reporter for the *Globe*, the *Mail*, and the *Toronto News*.

A year after he got his BA, the University of Toronto granted him the degree of bachelor of laws. King's mother cheered, for she wanted him to complete his professional training. King may have suspected that his father's place on the university senate contributed to the ease with which he got his law degree. Nonetheless, he acquired a third degree from Toronto in 1897 and an MA from Harvard, his fourth university degree in four years. And then he left law behind.

As for Pearson, he wrote: "The course of least resistance seemed to be to study law. . . ."

"I was duly articled, paid some fees, and began to study, as instructed, Anson's Law of Contract. This was the dullest book which I had ever read, and I was told I would have to read many more like it. . . . It occurred to me that I had no wish to become a man of law. In less than a week, the Supreme Court was deprived of a potential chief justice."

Joe Clark also had a narrow escape; the law turned its back on him.

Lawyers usually get rich, and most of our prime ministers do, too.

Mulroney and Clark had to worry about money, even though their parents were comfortably off by the standards of the 1930s, 1940s and 1950s. Mulroney's first mansion was the company president's house that the Iron Ore company gave him in Westmount; Clark's was Stornoway. He and Maureen moved in with scarcely a stick of furniture, an event rivaled in Ottawa only by the arrival of Ed and Lily Schreyer at Government House with plastic bags and the clothes they were wearing.

Shortage of cash was not a preoccupation in the private lives of King or Bennett or St. Laurent or Trudeau. Money and mansions were old stuff to them.

King's estate, not counting the value of Kingsmere, totalled almost $700,000. This included a subscription fund from wealthy Liberals for the upkeep of Laurier House ($225,000); a seventy-fourth birthday present from his patron, John D. Rockefeller, Jr. ($100,000); and a gift from Sir William Mulock ($50,000). King left Kingsmere and Laurier House to the nation; the Rockefeller gift went for graduate scholarships.

R.B. Bennett left an estate of 3.5 million, which surprised a lot of people who had thought it would be more because he always smelled of money.

Shortage of money bothered Diefenbaker. He tried not to let it show, and though his habits were frugal, he always managed to dress jauntily. Usually there was someone around to pick up the tab, and when his estate was probated it came to something over a million dollars, another surprise to a lot of people. His various executors are still tying to figure out who gets what.

Pearson's wife, Maryon, handled the family finances with some skill in the later years, providing a nest egg that the Nobel Prize money augmented nicely.

Trudeau was born rich and grew up richer. He seemed incapable of understanding what money worries were, either for people or for nations.

John Turner always seemed rich and talked and acted rich. But when he quit politics so abruptly in 1975, he confided to cabinet colleague Eugene Whelan: "Geez, Gene, I gotta make some money. My friends are all earning two hundred grand a year, and I don't intend to be an economic eunuch. I'm getting out of here."

"The themes of the Throne Speech are contemplation, rumination, meditation, and hesitation." – John Turner, 1984.

"And constipation." – Jean Chrétien.

Politicians relate to the world through their eloquence – or lack of it. Canadian prime ministers are always on their guard against saying anything as memorable as Chrétien's moment above, for fear of offending somebody somewhere.

In the United States leading political figures try to have something to say when they are on radio or TV; their Canadian counterparts count the program a success if they emerge without having said a damn thing.

When Lester Pearson was prime minister, he told me that he could feel the eyes of Mackenzie King burning into his with the awful message: "Don't do it, don't even say it!"

Not doing it turned out to be the chief bequest of King. Hence the belief that Canadian prime ministers get into trouble for sins of commission but not for sins of omission.

Avoiding deep water involves that central element of Canadian politics: compromise.

Some have used the word "conciliation."

Others have called it "flexibility."

Brian Mulroney sought to call it "civility," and even quested for "nobility."

Through the years we have heard phrases like "co-operative federalism," and "community of communities."

But not "appeasement." It's been a dirty word ever since Neville Chamberlain "appeased" Hitler.

All our prime ministers have had to appease somebody, though, or some region. All have appeased Quebec, in anglo eyes. All have appeased the anglos, in Quebec's eyes. And appeasement of Ontario is usually taken for granted, as that's where the votes (and everything else that isn't imported) come from.

The greatest appeaser of all was King.

He avoided commitment on anything, to the point where he lost the ability to commit. His conversation was a ride on a roundabout. His speeches were dreary, drawn-out non-statements. Once, lamenting the lack of a Canadian equivalent of the Gettysburg Address, we searched the speeches of King for a single sentence of the same brevity as Lincoln's speech. We failed to find one.

In fact, no words of any of our prime ministers live in the world's lexicon of important statements. The best we can muster is Laurier's, that the twentieth century would belong to Canada, or King's "conscription if necessary, but not necessarily conscription," or St. Laurent's words about the days of the supermen of Europe being over.

Speeches of two and three hours were still not unusual in St. Laurent's time, and before that there were no limits. King could go on for hours, stunning his hearers into a comatose state. His sentences and paragraphs knew no end. His main intent was to fuzzify, and he used a multiple-subject approach to achieve that aim.

Occasionally, however, he allowed himself to get to the point. When he watered the booze from eighty-six proof to seventy proof, he called on wartime Canadians to "put on the full armor of God" in the name of temperance; heavy drinking was impeding the war effort. But the real motive for diluting the liquor was to increase the tax take, which applied to the added water as well as to the alcohol. Provincial governments, watching the money roll in, have blessed his name to this day.

One of the few times King said what he meant he paid a price for it. In 1930, just before his defeat at the hands of Bennett's Tories, he declined to give the Tory provinces "a five-cent piece."

This was the wrong thing to say in the first year of the Great Depression.

Donald Brittain's 1988 CBC-TV miniseries about King caught something of King's tediousness while wisely avoiding the actual orations. The day after the series ended, I was talking to a young worker engaged in the latest enlargement and improvement of Kingsmere. "If this guy was such a boring old fart," he asked me, "why are we doing all this to glorify him?"

I was stuck for an answer, other than that, given our inclination to reject home-grown heroes, we have done far too little glorifying. The irony is that we should have chosen to exalt the least prepossessing of our leaders.

The contrast between the public-speaking styles of Meighen and King can be shown in a brief comparison. Meighen received the Freedom of the City of London in 1921, and King was accorded the same honor two years later. Their speeches each lasted five minutes (the required time limit) and both dealt with Empire.

Meighen, in part: "True it is that we share each other's security, and the peril of one is the peril of all; but subject to that consideration, our Dominions must determine their policies in the light of the conditions that surround them.

"What may be right for one may be entirely wrong for another. What may have been for you a mere passing care may be to us the most persistent and baffling problem of our politics."

Now for King: "True it is that in any minute survey of self-government as it exists in the constituent parts of the British Empire, there will be found forms and methods of procedure, customs and ceremonies, some of them venerated, others antiquated, which upon occasion may afford to the critics of British connection themes for discussion and debate. These are, however, outer trappings, in no way significant of the spirit of our constitution. They neither shackle nor bind. Where, at moments, they have occasioned irritation or a feeling of restraint, by a little mutual forbearance and common sense, a way to modify or change them has been quickly found. It is inevitable that as the British Dominions continue to increase in size, to grow in importance and influence, their freedom will, in all particulars, become commensurate with the extent of their interests."

King must have had his Guildhall audience dozing even more deeply than was its custom.

In a later speech King paid his respects to the Native peoples: "In the background of the present there remain the Indian habitations – the little groups of huts silhouetted against the forest depths, content to remain within its shadows that the larger Canada, emerging from obscurity and shade, may take her place in the sun among the powers of the world."

The Indians have been trying to figure that one out ever since.

King's gross verbal pomposity and obfuscation were at the heart of his dullness. At the outer edge was the fact that he was not a good enough actor, and years later Lester Person had the same problem when he appeared on television (a medium that King was spared).

Pearson's most significant political speech about Canada and the world, the one that unseated Diefenbaker and put the

Liberals in power for twenty-one years, was made to the York-Scarborough Liberal Association on January 12, 1963. (It was this speech that caused Pierre Trudeau to denounce him as the unfrocked pope of peace, creating the bad blood between them that lasted until Pearson's death.)

In this speech Pearson said that Canada should keep her commitments to adopt nuclear weapons, commitments that Diefenbaker denied were binding.

"In dealing with our friends," Pearson said, "we must assume that a change of government would not normally mean a sudden and unilateral renunciation of the treaty obligations they have undertaken. Our friends have the same right to assume that the commitments of Canada are the commitments of the nation; that they would not automatically disappear with a change of government."

(Twenty-five years later, Liberal leader John Turner would be promising to tear up any trade treaty that the Tory government might sign with the United States.)

It is thanks to Pearson that we have a record of a couple of his speeches to the annual Press Gallery dinner. Traditionally these talks are off the record, but on two occasions Pearson was prepared to let himself be quoted, begging forgiveness "for violating this sacred pledge, seeing that I am betraying only myself."

In the tenth and last of his gallery dinner addresses, he offered a wry summation of his political career: "My sixty days of decision were too decisive. I failed to get three maple leaves on the flag and I lost the blue border. I failed to get Vancouver into the NHL or Gabon into the Canadian confederation. I failed to realize that unification of the armed forces should have been preceded by unification of the cabinet. I was wrong in relying entirely on the Sermon on the Mount as the guideline for cabinet solidarity. But I treated these failures, as I did my successes, with a stoic and rather touching calm.

"So I leave you, with head held high, chins up, step steady, conscious of a job half done, confident also that the verdict of history will be: *Après lui, le déluge!*"

It was one of his most accurate predictions.

The Press Gallery dinners were also occasions for many of Pearson's off-the-record jokes and tales. One of his favorite stories was a report in London's *News of the World* that described the discovery of a dismembered female body in Hyde Park, detailing severed arms, legs, head, and other mutilations and ending with: "According to police, she had not been interfered with."

I remember one more he told, about the managing editor who was pressing for more stories from a reporter on assignment, only to have the city editor intervene, saying that the reporter only had two hands. Shouted the editor: "Well, fire the crippled bastard."

Pearson knew how to capture our attention informally, but his formal speeches were mostly dross. When the search was on for a pungent phrase to illuminate the lobby of the Lester B. Pearson building in Ottawa, nothing was found, and the carvers had to settle for a potted biography.

In my opinion, though, there was an appealing modesty to Pearson that informed his public speaking with a clarity and an impact the inflated Mackenzie King could never achieve. He was at his best in the Reith Lectures of 1969, a year after he had been replaced as prime minister. Two excerpts might have been worthy of the marble walls of the External Affairs building:

"The distinction between offensive and defensive arms was a very simple one. If you were in front of them, they were offensive; if you were behind them, they were defensive."

"It may well be that Wolfe's victory at Quebec not only made Canada safe for the British, at least for a time, but made the world safe for the American Revolution."

But Pearson was unable to rise emotionally to the occasion, and in this respect he resembled all our latter-day prime ministers except Diefenbaker. The closest Pearson ever came to expressing emotion was in his 1964 speech to the Royal Canadian Legion in Winnipeg defending his proposal for a distinctive Canadian flag:

"We who are elected to serve Canada in Parliament owe those who elect us more than the advocacy of non-controversial ideas. We owe Canada our best judgment, and we fail Canada if we fail to exercise that judgment, or if we pass our responsibility for judgment back to the electors who sent us to Parliament."

In his five years in office Pearson faced more issues than most government leaders, and most of his solutions were faulty. But the flag solution fulfilled his proudest hopes. It flew.

Some of Pierre Trudeau's lines were zingers like the one that the state has no place in the nation's bedrooms. On the stump and in the Commons he was hopeless unless goaded into a biting comeback. When he read a speech from text, he was awful.

In a prepared speech Joe Clark was the clearest of all, because high rhetoric just wasn't his style. But off the cuff he could sound silly, and those were the quotes that made it into the papers. Diefenbaker said of Joe: "The Tories celebrated the year of the child by electing one as leader."

The judgments history makes on our prime ministers depend as much on their foreign involvements as on their activities and abilities at home . . . at least, prime ministers like to think so.

Apart from Pearson's run at saving world peace, and Trudeau's jog over the same ground with side trips into the Eastern bloc and the Third World, Canada's foreign involvements have been mostly with Britain, the United States and, to a lesser extent, France.

Our leaders spent the first half of this century chipping away at the British tie while agonizing about the Canadian identity. The second half of the century they spent tightening the U.S. tie, content to let our agony over identity throb quietly.

Aware of the voters back home, all our PMs tried to sidle to the center of the world stage.

Mackenzie King valued his role as a founder of the United Nations. St. Laurent was a founder of the North Atlantic Treaty Alliance and a developer of the Commonwealth, and he put Canada into the foreign-aid business, so long as it contributed to our prosperity.

Pearson's action on Suez capped a career as our most successful diplomat. In a world where peace and honesty were hard to come by, he devised our role as peacemakers.

Diefenbaker claimed he tamed Nikita Khrushchev, and he was a leader in forcing the withdrawal of South Africa from the Commonwealth, while keeping his "light in the window." He fought for global disarmament. Though unsuccessful and receiving no credit, he felt he was entitled to a Nobel Peace Prize and was contemptuous of Pearson's claim. Despite his loathing for Communism, Diefenbaker established trade links with the People's Republic of China. And he used the British link in a vain effort to counter our nation's widening involvement with the United States.

Trudeau tried that same anti-U.S. ploy by seeking expanded ties with Europe and with anybody else who would deal with him, including the U.S.S.R. And he preached nuclear disarmament and north-south dialogue, though he advanced neither cause and risked humiliation in the process. In his eyes, however, he paved the way for *glasnost* and Gorbachev.

Canada rose in American esteem in Joe Clark's time when U.S. diplomats were given secret refuge in our embassy in Iran. The glow was short-lived, serving chiefly to propel Ambassador Ken Taylor into high-paying employment selling Shredded Wheat in New York and to complicate our own Middle Eastern policies.

Brian Mulroney has devoted most of his attention to strengthening the U.S. link, while bringing Canada into francophonie.

The British tie is virtually dead but our British inheritance is not. It shackles our politics, and has dogged the careers of every

one of our prime ministers. We couldn't have become a nation
without it, and now we can't get rid of it, because all our laws and
all our practices follow the British pattern and are enacted and
performed in the name of the Queen.

When the material ties with Britain wore thin, the emotional
tie was largely lost as well. The change started under Mackenzie
King, with the Americanization of our industrial economy.
Louis St. Laurent endorsed the idea that Canada could bridge
the two great western powers. Then we saw that the United
Kingdom wasn't a great power at all, and broke with Britain for
the first time over its invasion of Egypt in 1956.

A belated patriotic feeling for England swelled in some of us
after Suez and Lester Pearson's peace prize, and partly on the
strength of that feeling the St. Laurent government was
defeated and John Diefenbaker was elected prime minister.

Perhaps to mask his half German ancestry and certainly to
satisfy his suspicions of the United States, Diefenbaker
manifested strong pro-British sentiments, the last of our leaders
to do so. But the British government knocked these out of him
when they spurned his intention to divert 15 percent of
Canada's trade from the U.S. to the U.K. The British offered
instead complete free trade between Britain and Canada, and
Dief pulled back. The government in London developed a
distaste for Diefenbaker after that, though Whitehall's
subsequent scorn for Trudeau was stronger.

Once we had broken most of our British ties, we turned our
attention more and more to the Americans and to our place in
the supposed New World, the crucible in which our future PMs
will be tested. Yet most Canadians feel no sense of involvement
in hemispheric politics, cultures or languages. They are
indifferent, as they are to the emergence of Japan as our new
economic "mother country."

12. Conjugal Wrongs

"Behind every successful man, there is a surprised woman."
                                        – *Maryon Pearson*

Neither Mackenzie King nor R.B. Bennett married, but both were stimulated and subsidized by women.

Olive Diefenbaker kept her husband sane when he was under extreme stress.

Maryon Pearson increased the stresses on her man.

Margaret Trudeau drove her husband to near distraction.

Maureen McTeer propelled Joe Clark to the prime ministership but couldn't sustain him there and called their joint tenure a trip to hell times three.

Geills Turner saved Vancouver Quadra for her husband, but his prime ministership was gone.

Mila Mulroney was Brian's biggest potential asset, but her style for style's sake brought critics down on her, and she retreated into Mulroney's shadow, leaving the impression that his inner circle was a male bastion.

Our married prime ministers, by and large, have not been helped overmuch by their wives. Pearson, Trudeau and Clark married strong-willed women who worked against the grain of their supposed pre-liberation role, each insisting on being her own person, each developing a constituency of her own at the expense of her husband's public support.

Feminism has had a significant effect on Ottawa wives, though much remains to be achieved. When she was mayor of Ottawa, Charlotte Whitton pointed out that a woman has to be at least three times as good as a man to succeed, adding that this was not all that difficult. And as the Parliamentary Spouses Association points out, voters get two for the price of one when they elect MPs; the spouse of the member of Parliament toils in common cause without pay or recognition.

The spouses of our diplomats on foreign postings have long argued against the lack of reward for jobs at least as demanding as their mates'. Some have simply refused to share the joys and hardships of foreign postings, telling their spouses to go it alone, or find another line of work or another mate.

MPs' mates have also been known to reject the political life – one reason politics takes such a heavy toll of marriages. . .nearly as heavy as that graveyard of relationships, the national media.

Some spouses have made themselves an asset, but most would rather be elsewhere, and many scarcely visit Ottawa at all, while their mates, male MPs usually, share apartments like monks or reborn teenagers. Deputy Prime Minister Don Mazankowski has maintained such a *pied-à-terre* in Ottawa for twenty years.

The role of the political spouse is obviously still evolving. The latest quirk is the inclusion of spouses in the conflict-of-interest legislation. Jane Crosbie, wife of John, has told the government not to stick its nose into her personal finances, and it would have been fun to watch the fireworks had her husband made it to 24 Sussex. More and more spouses of MPs share her view. Including me.

The early Mrs. Diefenbaker, Edna, was a down-to-earth woman who had a circle of friends in Ottawa, but it was a circle without style. She did have a fey sense of humor and tried to pep things up for her husband, who wasn't much of a party animal.

She took well to the life of an MP's wife in Ottawa, doing the rounds of teas and card parties and keeping a series of modest apartments neat. During the Depression she suggested she take up teaching again to add to John's meager income from the law, but on his mother's advice he insisted that no wife of his should ever work.

Diefenbaker leaned more on his mother than on any other woman until Olive Evangeline Freeman Palmer came back into his life right after Edna's death in 1951.

Olive submerged herself in the role of John's wife, assuming a sweet smile in public, through good times and bad. Great at wakes and weddings, at bazaars and tea parties and platform appearances, she received more bouquets of flowers than any other woman in Canada. A composed woman, she wasn't given to kicking up her heels; her one big passion was ice cream. Diefenbaker would hold up any parade or procession if he saw a chance to get a cone for Olive. And for himself.

Dief's heart was on the prairies, but Olive's was in western Ontario; Ottawa was definitely an afterthought in her life. Nevertheless, she agreed to be buried there, and Diefenbaker's uprooting of her remains to be buried alongside his in Saskatoon was done without her agreement. At least her final resting place acknowledges her role in the nation's affairs. Edna is buried on the far side of Saskatoon.

Sweet Olive had her opposite in sour-faced Maryon Pearson, who hated political Ottawa. Or perhaps it was just that she regarded politics as a waste of her husband's time and talents. She was in many ways brighter than Pearson, and she enlivened his few off hours with caustic comments about politicians, including him. Occasionally she sought solace in libations that, far from mellowing her, aroused her brittle temperament to verbal violence and dish throwing. She chain-smoked, using a long cigarette holder, inhaling so deeply her eyes bulged and watered. And always she let it be known that the role of prime-ministerial wife was a bore. Whenever she could, she hid from it and from the social rituals that official Ottawa thrust at her.

At the height of the 1966 scandals that plagued the government of her husband, Maryon Pearson said the media was ganging up on him.

"The newspapers are always at the poor old prime minister," she complained, wondering why no one could find something nice to say. She mused how marvelous it would be if all the newspaper editors formed a government, then everybody would see just how well *they* ran the country.

It wasn't just what we wrote about her husband that she resented. She said that we tended to knock all things Canadian, that if anything had Canadian content we assumed there must be something wrong with it.

For all her early disdain of politics, Maryon Pearson was the last prime-ministerial wife to attend Commons sessions and sit in the Visitors' Gallery and follow the proceedings closely.

Like Olive Diefenbaker she was a regular in the gallery. It was not unusual for cabinet and parliamentary wives to be on hand in the Commons back then, either to keep informed or to egg their husbands on. Perhaps this is so rare nowadays because parliamentary wives have become more political in their own right. Maryon Pearson might approve of such a development, though it's likely she'd say she couldn't care less.

Maryon's lasting contribution to social custom was the abolition of the curtsy at Government House. She said she'd be damned if she was going to bend her knee to that bitch Norah Michener.

During Roland Michener's time as speaker, Norah had taken it upon herself to hold seminars on manners and protocol for the wives of MPs, most of whom were married to Tories new to politics, following the Diefenbaker landslide of 1958.

Norah was an authority on the right and wrong way of doing

things, and while some parliamentary wives valued her teachings, others found her unbearably stuffy. I shared the latter view until I found her stumping the walkways of Parliament Hill, trying to stir up support for her out-of-work husband following the 1962 election in which he lost his seat and his speakership. She grabbed me by the lapels and barked: "Are you going to let that bastard [Diefenbaker] get away with what he's doing to my Roly?"

A woman who'd go to bat for her man like that couldn't be all stuffy.

Pearson retired just a year after he appointed Michener to Government House, and the two women then merely had to inhabit the same city.

When Michener asked for his autobiography to be done in the form of a television documentary, I was the on-camera host. The program was first screened at Government House, and I found myself seated in the audience beside Norah Michener and Mrs. Pearson. As scenes unfolded of Mrs. Michener running state affairs at Rideau Hall and at the residence in the Citadel in Quebec, Mrs. Pearson became increasingly restless. She finally muttered to the First Lady, "You seem to have got more than your share of attention in this thing."

Silence from Mrs. Michener.

"Did you ask to have your picture taken?"

Silence.

"When the CBC did their program on Mike, they didn't ask me to come in."

Silence.

"Not a single picture of me. Not even a mention."

At this point Governor-General Michener leaned across his wife and gave Mrs. Pearson a reassuring pat, mumbling, "There, there, my dear."

"Don't 'there, there' me," said Mrs. Pearson through clenched teeth. "If it hadn't been for my husband, you'd be practising law in Toronto!"

And as the lights went up, Mrs. Pearson left.

It is one of fate's ironies that these two strong-minded women spent their last days in the same nursing home outside Toronto, each unaware of the other's presence.

After Maryon, Margaret. But we had to wait a long time for her.

In the years between Trudeaumania and Trudeau's marriage, the press speculated wildly about whom he should marry and when. The media assumed that marriage would mellow him and make our jobs easier.

Trudeau claimed he'd been unable to settle down in the thirty years of his adult life because he was such an agreeable man he didn't want to hurt the many by choosing the one.

We tried to matchmake for him by suggesting prominent and eligible women of the time, including Princess Kahn Tineta Horn and Trudeau's former colleague in the Pearson government Judy LaMarsh. Horn showed no interest, and LaMarsh disqualified herself by describing Trudeau as an arrogant bastard who regarded women as mere toys and decorative bits of fluff.

Trudeau had a series of unique – for a prime minister – relationships with women, both before and after his marriage. He said that if he ever felt like giving up on Canada, he would go to New York, "where the action is."

Fellow partygoers told of Pierre's exultation at being in a city like New York, where nobody cared who he was, or, as he put it, where "I can walk along and do anything. . .pick my nose if I like." Only Trudeau would seek anonymity wearing a bone-white trench coat with Barbra Streisand on his arm and her press agents beating every drum in town.

Madam Helma, the owner of the bistro known as Casa Brazil, was thrilled to have Miss Streisand at her place but assumed Trudeau was some unknown actor. When Barbra introduced the PM, Helma said to Barbra, "You have a very nice man there." Pierre and Barbra dined on beef Wellington and roast duck, and we never discovered who paid the bill – Trudeau never having been known to pick up a tab in his life. (It was his boast that he never carried money and had no credit cards.) We were told only that Trudeau had made the reservation at Casa Brazil two weeks earlier and that Helma had to provide a nearby table for security personnel from the RCMP, the U.S. State Department, and the New York City police.

Trudeau had said, at the time of his earlier involvement with Miss Eva Rittenhausen (who'd shot her mouth off about him), that he didn't welcome publicity about his private life. When a companion gave interviews, he said, "I re-adjust my friendships or acquaintances according to these discoveries."

The Hill scene was the public climax of the Streisand affair. We were left to wonder, as much now as then, what it was they did in private, and what they talked about. Did she sing to him, did they play her records, did he give her long discourses on philosophy? Did they do yoga? Did she talk show business? Did they talk about religion, and if so, what did they say? (As Streisand later sang: "Would a convent take a Jewish girl?")

During Barbra's visit to the House of Commons, Vic Chapman and British Columbia's Gordon Gibson were her bodyguards and kept us media minions at bay. At one point she was heard to answer a reporter with, "No, not yet." When I begged to know what the question had been, I was told it was whether Pierre had taken her snowmobiling.

When she was finally out of the building and on her way to 24 Sussex Drive, we asked Chapman what his next move was. He said he was going to help Gibson climb back upstairs.

The whole affair led nowhere, and it turned out Trudeau had child Margaret hidden in an attic somewhere up at the lake. But, God, it was fun while it lasted, and we in the press corps were never the same again.

Some time later we learned that at the beginning of the relationship Barbra had felt headed for high places in Canada. She began reading for the role, boning up on what her share of power in Canada might involve and even starting French lessons.

No less than Barbra, Margaret was a source of wonder to

Ottawa, as indeed she was to the nation and eventually to the world. After a time as Trudeau's "country mistress" at Harrington Lake, she married into politics without having the faintest idea what would be required of her and turning up her pretty nose when she found out.

When I chided her that as the daughter of a leading federal politician and cabinet minister she should have had prior knowledge, she said she had hated her father and all his works until she was in her twenties, so I wasn't to give her any of "that crap." (Jimmy Sinclair was a hell of a nice guy, a darling of the Press Gallery.)

Margaret was more at home in Marrakech or New York or Toronto or Paris – anywhere that jets could carry her. Apart from a small neighborhood circle of eccentric women friends, all rebelling against mandarin marriages, she found official Ottawa stuffy beyond endurance.

She refused the traditional perch atop the pyramid of wifely power and threw the whole structure askew, so nobody knew where to sit or whom to defer to or smile at. "You're upsetting the apple cart," I told her, and she said, "Goody, goody!"

At 24 Sussex Drive she opened all the windows and blew out pot smoke, to the consternation of the Mounties on guard below. She hated that house. She turned an upstairs room into a refuge from her personal demons – and Pierre's.

Later she hid from his visiting women friends. And he gave her a shiner for her antics with Mick Jagger and the Stones.

After the marriage ended, she joined ordinary onlookers at great events. During a royal visit, there she was, the Trudeau kids in tow, on the fringe of a crowd watching the Queen go to church around the corner from the house Margaret shared with her then lover.

Margaret eventually remarried, settled down and became a model young matron, so low profile that she doesn't even return a wave from old media pals and tormentors. Having tried – and failed – at photography and television and movies, she found peace in the capital city.

Maureen McTeer is as interesting as Margaret, but whereas Margaret was a hangover from the flower-child era, McTeer is ahead of her time.

Once, in High River, Alberta, I heard the chairman of a function refer to Joe's wife as "Maureen Clark." High River was the only town in Canada where anybody would dare make such an error.

Maureen's insistence on retaining her family name, now such a commonplace thing to do, harmed Joe Clark in the eyes of many. Referring to her home village downriver from Ottawa, one politically minded Ottawa judge asked: "If [Joe] can't handle that blister from Cumberland, how in hell can he run the country?"

Without McTeer's drive I am certain Clark would never have aspired to, let alone attained, the leadership of the Progressive Conservative Party. Once he won it, three things emerged to general surprise: one, that he was a Catholic; two, that he had made himself bilingual; and three, that he was married to McTeer.

The religious thing no longer matters in Canadian politics; the Mulroneys, the Turners, the Sauvés are all Catholic. Clark's bilingualism, a rare accomplishment for an Albertan at the time, came to be seen as an aberration. And McTeer, while determined to preserve a life of her own, gradually made concessions to official expectations. She spruced up her wardrobe and acquired a style and taste that left her old Cumberland image far behind.

But though she bears the scars of her husband's brief term in office, she is still speaking out on heritage causes and the arts and publicly advocating abortion on demand. When she won the nomination to run as the Conservative candidate in the Ottawa riding of Carleton-Gloucester, there was Joe by her side, in the hall where he won his leadership a dozen years earlier and lost it seven years after.

Other PMs have tried to adapt to new feminist realities, but they seemed to come to Joe naturally. In fact, he addressed the issue of equal rights with an ease and fluency that he showed on no other subject.

His attitude may have been shaped by McTeer or by his mother, but it could never have come from the social environment in which he was raised. The businesses of Alberta are oil and wheat and ranching, all three of them dominated, then as now, by men.

Critics who carped at McTeer's frugal ways mocked Mila Mulroney's extravagance. If McTeer had not had enough shoes, then Mila had too many. If McTeer's first garden party ran out of food and booze, at Mila's the whiskey and champagne flowed like buttermilk.

When criticized, McTeer cried tears of rage. Mila cried, too, but out of anguish, partly for her husband and partly for herself – until she learned to crinkle her nose and busy herself bringing up the kids and looking after Brian, a wifely role that earned the scorn of feminists, presumably McTeer among them, though Maureen never said as much.

Maureen is now popular in Ottawa for doing her shopping there. Mila, too, shops in Ottawa, for all the fuss made about her sprees in Montreal, Toronto, and New York.

But Mila-bashing is less about where she shops than how much she spends. Take, for example, what happened at 24 Sussex.

During the Mulroneys' short spell in opposition, Mila cultivated an Italian designer called Giovanni Mowinckel, and together they transformed drab Stornoway into a showplace. When Mila and Brian moved to the PM's mansion on Sussex Drive, Mowinckel came along, and his work was just as stunning. He became the toast of the town and was asked to design, among other things, the new Rideau Club premises, where he created what is thought to be the most pleasing of all posh highrise clubs in the country. But he got too big for his boots, and he and Mila had a parting of the ways. He fled to his native Italy, leaving behind a string of unsettled debts.

Soon, abandoned employees started leaking Mowinckel's secrets to Stevie Cameron of the *Globe and Mail*, and the story was out about irresponsible spending on renovations.

The stories neglected to say that a firm of consulting engineers had first reported the house in dire need of repairs – in danger of burning down if the roof didn't cave in first.

The famous Trudeau indoor swimming pool was found to have been badly built and badly installed, causing everything around it to rot.

"This residence is now considered a national monument," said the consultants, "and as such should reflect the position of the highest elected official in the land."

Fact is, though, 24 Sussex is merely one of many Ottawa mansions put up by the lumber barons in the days when timbering was more important than governing. (Many of these mansions, much more splendid than 24 Sussex, flourish as foreign embassies on the rule of thumb that the poorer the country, the bigger the embassy.)

The consultants recommended spending $600,000 to fix it up, and there's been howling ever since – from the occupants about what needs to be repaired and from the critics about the cost.

Ironically, Mulroney was criticized for being in conflict of interest with his party because he borrowed money from party funds to finance some remodeling; then it was suggested that Mulroney might be in conflict with the Income Tax Act for not reporting the loan. But eventually the public wearied of the game, Brian and Mila were happy with the carpets at last (they were allegedly replaced three times to get the color match) and nobody lost any more sleep over the issue.

The next hot topic was the Mulroneys' wardrobe, as if the

Mulroneys were Ferdinand and Imelda Marcos. But the Mulroneys' lifestyle is simply that of the head of the Iron Ore Company, when the firm provided the perks. Similarly, John Turner's Toronto apartment, paid for by the Liberals, is an effort to preserve the luxury he had known as a big-shot Toronto lawyer.

Susan Riley's 1988 book on political wives was a hatchet job on Mila. (Riley has said that she thought of calling it *Talk Softly and Marry a Big Prick.*) Riley is only one of the many taking shots at Mila for her big spending, wifely subservience and abuse of her position. Mulroney deflected a lot of the criticism by drawing fire to himself. But in 1987 he sat silent in the House of Commons during the opposition attack on his wife for forwarding a letter from French teacher Georges Grossmann to the minister of state for immigration, Gerry Weiner.

The minister countered that members of Parliament intervene in immigration cases all the time, and produced immigration case files from Mila's chief tormentors, Liberal Sergio Marchi and New Democrats Nelson Riis and Ed Broadbent. But with disgruntled immigration workers providing some of the ammunition through their union and the NDP, it took a week for the parliamentary heat to move off Mila Mulroney. As a media event the affair overshadowed the francophone summit in Quebec City, which the prime minister had touted as one of the major achievements of his government. It was one more custard pie in the face: the Sinclair Stevens débâcle took attention away from the visit to China, and slap-happy Sondra Gotlieb's headline grabber fouled his summit visit to Washington.

Yet all Mila did was forward a letter that one of her kids had brought home from teacher.

When Nancy Reagan came to town with the president in 1987, Mila Mulroney threw a luncheon for her and invited a select handful of media people. Mila spoke briefly, saying that both she and Nancy were graduates of the school of hard knocks. (Maureen McTeer, who was present, could have told both of them something about that.) Mila said that the wives of leaders were as accountable as their husbands. And she described Nancy as her best friend.

Nancy Reagan talked through lunch with her table mates, cartoonist Ben Wicks and shoe tycoon Sonja Bata, which must have given her an interesting idea of Canadian accents.

I thought it was a swell affair that did our side proud, but I felt for the some seventy-five security officers who had to stand around unfed, and for the media hordes who fulminated outside the closed doors.

My own inclination, even before I got invited to the lunch, was to regard Mila Mulroney as Yugoslavia's answer to Raisa Gorbachev – she is one of our national bright spots, along with the Mulroney kids, who deserve to be seen at least as much as Trudeau's offspring were.

Brian Mulroney is very lucky in his wife. Of course, Brian doesn't appreciate just how lucky. He brought gobs of machismo into the marriage, along with carloads of cronies. Croneyism tends to accentuate manhood at the expense of womankind. Not one of Mulroney's hundreds of pals is a woman, and his storytelling, his blarney, is male-oriented. As none of his media buddies – all carefully cultivated over the years – is a woman, he became vulnerable to the new media women, who vastly outnumber his reporter pals. They wasted no time in ruthlessly heaping scorn on his old-boy network.

One-time press groupie Brian Mulroney contends that he no longer reads what is said of him, just as Trudeau didn't, and he has been spending his spare time enjoying Trudeau's pool, reminding himself, no doubt, that he first spotted the tall, tanned Mila Pivnicki beside a swimming pool and said: "That's for me!"

Since 1961, when I publicly pronounced that Canadian women were better than their men in every way, I have seen a number of important changes in the status of women in this country.

There are more women working everywhere in what you

could call the mainstream or the rat race. But what I didn't foresee back in 1961, and what all our PMs except for Clark have had trouble coping with since then, are "women's issues." Women have an equal stake with men in all political, international, economic, scientific and artistic matters, but on issues such as abortion and day care, they claim special interest, as they do in the fight for equal rights and equal pay for work of equal value.

In Lester Pearson's time women chained themselves to seats in the Commons galleries and shouted their demands at the MPs below. Commons guards were issued wire cutters so the protestors could be ejected.

Today women are involved in every aspect of Canadian public life. It sometimes seems that all the learned media commentators on economics, trade, medicine and politics are named Barbara or Deborah or Diane. As one who grew up in an age when a newspaperwoman's place was on the society page, I applaud the emergence of females in our newspaper rooms and as anchors and hosts of radio and TV shows.

I was there when Pierre Trudeau was first faced with Barbara Frum, on a CBC-TV panel show early in the 1960s. None of us had ever heard of her. She was nominated by CBC-Toronto to be part of the panel, and Trudeau tried to give her the new-girl-in-town treatment. His tone implied that she knew nothing about politics and economics. It turned out she knew a great deal about both, and in the intervening twenty years her kind of questioning and her liberal views have set the tone for women in public affairs journalism in Canada. Her run has been longer than Trudeau's, and it can be argued that her influence on events in Canada has been almost as great. On journalism it has been much greater.

I look forward to hearing a lot more from women, particularly Mila Mulroney.

Mila hasn't said much in public, but whenever she does, she

comes across well. At a banquet for Ottawa restaurateur and man-about-town Dave Smith, she faced the crowd and said any Tory would be glad to see so many people. And she thanked Smith for keeping Brian's photograph on the wall of his popular downtown bistro, even though he had moved it from the dining room to the kitchen.

"At 22 percent in the polls," she said, "what could a Tory expect?"

13. The PM and the Boys

"The profession of politics is held in very, very low esteem by the people of our country, away below sportsmen, actors, and everybody else. I suppose the explanation perhaps is that in a sense we are paid to belittle each other."   – *Pierre Trudeau*

"Fuck off," said Pierre Trudeau in the House of Commons on a February day in 1971.

In fact, he said it three times, addressing the remark to John Lundrigan, James McGrath and Lincoln Alexander of the Tory opposition.

The first stopped Lundrigan in the middle of a question about unemployment. He said he didn't understand what the prime minister had just asked him to do.

At this point McGrath jumped in and yelled at Trudeau: "Shame on you! Say it for *Hansard*."

Mr. Speaker Lucien Lamoureux asked what was being complained of.

Lincoln Alexander rose to his feet and said: "He used this four-letter word twice and then looked at me and used the same word again. Shameful and unacceptable! A gesture like this with the finger, there is no question what it means."

Outside the House Trudeau explained that what he had said was "fuddle-duddle," which led McGrath publicly to refer to him as "Fuddly-dud." McGrath charged that Trudeau, by trying to cover up what he'd really said, wanted to be "obscene but not heard." (Two of the three MPs became lieutenant-governors of their provinces – Alexander in Ontario and McGrath in Newfoundland. Nobody tells them to fuck off now.)

Almost every day a prime minister must face powerful forces officially sworn to take issue with him. These people are on the public payroll to prevent him from doing what he is on the public payroll to do.

In the House of Commons elected enemies often express their displeasure in petty ways, such as name calling and sneering; but swearing is unacceptable in the House, though libel is not.

Sometimes animosity turns into open hostility or, worse, into paranoid suspicion. John Diefenbaker was one PM who really knew how to hate. He had a lengthy hate list and an abiding distrust of just about everybody. Here was a man with all the qualities of leadership, yet he let himself be consumed by a fear of his colleagues and a loathing of his adversaries.

Before entering politics Diefenbaker had never run anything more complex than a small prairie law office. When he became an MP, he labored for years in opposition. His managerial inexperience and all that time attacking the government had warped his perspective by the time his turn finally came.

He despised Mike Pearson, and the feeling came to be reciprocated. This mutual enmity drained their energies and clouded their prime ministries. Diefenbaker would have been a better PM if Pearson hadn't been around. Pearson certainly would have been a better PM without Diefenbaker to confound him. Each worked assiduously to ensure the failure of the other, and each succeeded. What should have been a battle between giants was often more like little boys hurling spitballs.

The Mike and Dief war is a consequence of a parliamentary system that makes as much of opposition rights as Canada's system does. The parliamentary gun has long been loaded in favor of the elected enemies, and the enemies have acquired more power to impede government than any elected opposition in the world. We are spared violent coups, but verbal ones bring Parliament to its knees.

Opposition strength has kept us free of tyranny, but it has also kept us free of strong and effective government.

I have seen good governments made bad by "effective" opposition whose effectiveness in terms of the public good has not been apparent. Besides the damage Pearson and Diefenbaker did to each other's administrations, I think of Arthur Meighen brought down by Mackenzie King, and Joe Clark brought down by Liberal schemers.

By the same token the long periods of Liberal rule, thought by some to be the best and brightest periods in our politics, coexisted with oppositions that were *not* effective - Manion *versus* King, Bracken *versus* King, Drew *versus* St. Laurent, Stanfield *versus* Trudeau.

Our system is copied from the British. They, however, have taken pains throughout the centuries to ensure that British governments in office have a chance to govern, and that Parliament has a chance to work and not merely impede. No Canadian government would ever dare to promote its own interests in the manner of successive British regimes.

Any PM in Canada who tries to get away with declaring government information his personal property, as Trudeau did - calling those who sought such information "thieves" -

deserves all the opposition we can throw at him. But how the adversarial process works in this country – and especially how it works for television, where a criticism of policy often becomes more compelling than the policy – can only misguide and eventually dispirit our citizenry.

I sympathize with our recent PMs' impatience at much of what passes for opposition. The elected enemies, grandstanding for the idiot box, are becoming increasingly tiresome. My sympathy was with Speaker John Bosley, as recorded by *Hansard*:

> Petition: That MPs of all parties should stop name-calling, sarcastic put-downs, and bad language in the House of Commons.
> Speaker John Bosley: "Send it here so I can check it."
> Clerk: "It has been checked."
> Mr. Speaker: "I know – this is just my way of getting it up here so I could sign it!"

John F. Kennedy said that the presidency was a poor place for making new friends, so he wanted to keep a few of his old ones.

Canadian prime ministers have shown more or less the same desire, depending on how many friends they had to begin with.

Pierre Trudeau needed friends least, being content with his own company and counsel. Brian Mulroney needs friends most and started out as a networker in his earliest days in Baie Comeau, nourishing relationships throughout his youth, his college days, his practice of law, and his years as a back-room politician. He has sought to keep these old "friends," estimated at around four hundred.

It would be hard to imagine Pierre Trudeau even remembering that many names. The few friends he appears to cherish have said that the man remains a mystery, the most private public person they've ever known.

Both the introverted Trudeau and the extroverted Mulroney

have used people for their own ends in very different ways. Trudeau sees friendship as function: according to him, personal relationships were great when there was a shared working cause but hard to maintain after.

Even such supposed intimates as Jean Marchand and ex-journalist Gérard Pelletier felt a wall between them and the inner Trudeau, and their relationships with him flourished when work needed to be done or decisions made.(I asked Trudeau to elaborate on his views of friendship, but he declined, saying only that too many books were being written.)

Mulroney's friendships were also formed in the work atmosphere and cultivated with incessant telephone calls and get-togethers. Hundreds of colleagues believed that they were among his nearest and dearest, as he kept telling them they were. They, in turn, valued the relationship, if only for the outside chance that the man's ambition to be prime minister might be realized, in which case there would be favors to be sought and received.

Maybe it's Mulroney's nouveau-riche insecurity and his ambition that make him believe he has to have a huge host of close pals. If so, take away the game of politics and what is left? But, Mulroney might add, what more is needed?

All of us have faced changes in our friendships during our working lives, and those who have retired know just how quickly social ties can break as well. It's been said that a person is lucky to have two or three true friends in a lifetime (and journalists tend to have fewer than that if they are any good at their job).

But politicians never know for sure who their friends are. Some of the knives coming at them are being thrown by sworn allies. Every friend is a self-seeker to some degree. All a prime minister has to do to test this thesis is lose an election.

Brian Mulroney has yet to learn this lesson. He continues to carry gregariousness to an extreme. He can barely stand solitude, and if no cronies are on hand, he chats on the phone endlessly, sometimes through the night.

Is this true?

Mulroney thinks not.

I caught him on the fly, on his way to the movies with his four children, baby Nicholas on his lap in the limo, Mountie cars fore and aft, summer crowds craning for a look.

He kept them all waiting while we discussed friendship, and he mocked media for saying that what he had weren't friends, but cronies.

"In the pejorative sense," he bristled.

What would he call them?

"Friends. True, valued, loyal and genuine friends."

Did he need people like that around, to talk to?

"No I don't do that. There's a lot of myths about."

Do friends stay friends when they join the official circle?

"The relationship is not what it was when we were all practising law together, or when we were all in law school. There is a different relationship. It retains its mutual respect."

But surely friendship is more than mutual respect?

"Oh, absolutely."

Does he still fish with his friends?

"When I have the spare time I don't go fishing with them any more. I take the kids to the movies. With that and having them around for meetings at the house, and on airplanes, and in the office, we perhaps see more of our children than other parents in similar circumstances. Lookit, time is so precious, and there's not enough of it."

With that, they all went off to see *Bambi*.

Mulroney is not the first prime minister to be addicted to the telephone. John Diefenbaker was always on the blower to his private and ever-changing group of confidants across the country. But despite his phenomenal memory for names and faces, and his hearty jokes and anecdotes, Diefenbaker was essentially a loner. Not as self-sufficient as Trudeau – he required yes-men and yes-women around to sustain his high opinion of himself – he was nevertheless a private man who preferred his own company and that of his wife, Olive.

Trudeau, though infatuated with his child bride, treated Margaret as an intruder in the important business of running the country. He resented the publicity she attracted and eventually alienated her. He showed not the slightest sign of emotion in public at her subsequent behavior.

Only in the presence of children – his own and other people's – does he turn sentimental: "Truth, beauty, these make me rejoice. And you find that in a child – that creativity, the being forming itself, learning to live. And I marvel to see all this." However, he also admitted that as a child he must have been a pain in the ass.

Trudeau's idea of friendship made it easy for him to adjust to the loneliness of high office; Mulroney's warmer approach gets him into trouble, first because he surrounds himself with cronies and then because he has to jettison them.

The loss of personal relationships is common among those in high places, in any field of endeavor. But corporate czars, judges and bishops can at least fraternize with one another.

There are precious few people whom those at the pinnacles of political power can turn to for talk among equals. Maybe this explains the proliferation of summit meetings. Even the withdrawn Trudeau cherished his meetings with Helmut Schmidt and Third World leaders. Mulroney treasures his relationships with Helmut Kohl, Ronald Reagan and Margaret Thatcher. It wasn't just that he enjoyed strutting on the world stage – every prime minister has enjoyed that. He genuinely looked forward to the company of Thatcher and other summiteers in Toronto in June 1988.

Pearson was one of the most down-to-earth men ever to head a government, yet even he kept a part of himself aloof, and he had few intimates, political or otherwise. When he announced his intention to retire, virtually every cabinet colleague abandoned him in order to establish rival candidacies for leadership, and the business of governance was put on hold while the competitors fought among themselves for his succession.

Joe Clark was almost as isolated as Pearson, but lacked Pearson's background of global achievements. Joe's winning of the Tory leadership was not due to a broad circle of friends and cronies, any more than Pearson's elevation had been. A majority of Clark's former cabinet colleagues supported him against Mulroney because they resented the intruder from Montreal and his outriders. Once in office, Mulroney simply incorporated the entire enemy camp into his vast circle of friends and flattered them silly, telling them to hold tight in the bad times and the good times would come.

John Turner is another networker. He claims to have kept a mental note of the 195 last-ballot delegates who voted for him as leader in 1968 and harbors a soft spot for many who went to university with him or practised law with him or served beside him in cabinet or fawned on him during his moneymaking years in the Toronto boardrooms.

It is hard to imagine Mackenzie King "networking" or sharing confidences with anybody or anything other than his dog and his diary. Only Franklin D. Roosevelt called him Mackenzie, and one or two people in his later life called him Rex. He had no need of friendships and was suspicious of those who did. He listened to "voices," not people.

So, it emerged, did that other public recluse – Pierre Trudeau.

Trudeau argued with his voices that February night when he walked in the blizzard. He finally accepted their advice that it was time to go, but he took no earthly counsel.

14. Holy Mother Corp

"I need to know what is going on, and what is going wrong in my government. . . ."   – *Joe Clark*

Television, often hailed as the greatest of man's achievements, was also mourned as "the light that failed."

In the news and public affairs arena, where the art of politics is played before the public, TV trivializes the issues and reduces the participants to showbiz celebrities. At its worst, TV news presents politicians as guilty until proven innocent.

With the introduction of television into the House of Commons, Parliament has become a charade, a situation comedy, a sad parody of a democratic process that once valued debate as a meaningful part of government. I once campaigned in favor of TV in the House, hoping that it would improve the level of debate and public understanding. But vast sums are spent on broadcasting to an indifferent audience the same old acrimonious drivel that passes for parliamentary exchange and on archiving it for a presumably indifferent posterity.

Canadian politicians' relationship with television is a special one, since it involves our own unique TV service, the Canadian Broadcasting Corporation/Radio Canada. The CBC, in its news and public affairs programming, represents the most glaring example of a government voting public money to sustain the instrument of its own torment, if not destruction.

The roll call of prime ministers who have bemoaned the CBC dates back to St. Laurent, who tried to tame it but couldn't.

Diefenbaker felt the CBC was plotting against him. (Once it may have been. Someone sabotaged Diefenbaker's teleprompter script by deleting the letter "M" whenever it appeared. After he'd stumbled through the broadcast, the prime minister demanded disciplinary action, but the corporation blamed it all on a technical hitch.)

Pearson felt the CBC was a plot against the country.

Trudeau said that Radio Canada was an agency of Quebec separatism.

Joe Clark's government died at the hands of the CBC. (Clark himself was more the victim of print punditry.)

John Turner, boosted into leadership by plugs on CBC, was then knocked dead by CBC ridicule.

Brian Mulroney would sell the network to the highest bidder if he dared.

Diefenbaker tried to reform it; Pearson tried to change the rules and Trudeau made one of his pet cronies president to subdue it. Mulroney is still trying to figure out what to do about it.

But the CBC is bigger than all of them.

The opposition parties made sure no elected government could prevail in a tangle with the publicly funded CBC. As long as it had the favor and support of the other side of the House, the CBC could stand up with impunity to any government. Consequently, the opposition has always received extensive air time, and the anti-government bias shows on air.

Lester Pearson collided with the CBC repeatedly. He attempted to defuse the corporation's antagonism by changing the Broadcasting Act, and he encouraged his secretary of state, Judy LaMarsh, to put her appointees atop the CBC's executive structure. It didn't work.

When Patrick Watson and Laurier LaPierre sought to establish what amounted to a revolutionary regime through the program *This Hour Has Seven Days*, Prime Minister Pearson had the program squelched. At the time of death the show's sensation-a-week technique had built an audience of more than three million Canadians.

The CBC lost that battle, but they won the war: never again would a government go head-on against the electronic talking heads it paid for. And never would the talking heads lean the government's way and risk the charge of producing paid propaganda.

The one politician who might have known how to bring the CBC around to his point of view was Pierre Trudeau. He was made for TV, and it for him. So strong was his impact on screen that he was able to carry the CBC for a while. On-camera cynics – even Patrick Watson – were turned into pussycats.

Trudeau's crucial confrontation with Quebec Premier Daniel Johnson happened during the first federal-provincial conference to be shown on TV. Sitting beside Lester Pearson, Trudeau challenged Johnson's Quebec nationalism and in five minutes won the cheers of most English-speaking Canadians.

His way with television wrecked the hopes of his rivals for the Liberal leadership and launched the mania that shattered Conservative Leader Robert Stanfield in 1968. Stanfied moaned: "I've been on the CBC before . . . once or twice during the last election."

Yet even Trudeau ran into grief with the CBC. During the FLQ crisis the whole country saw that impromptu outdoor debate on the steps of the Parliament buildings between CBC's Tim Ralfe and Trudeau. How far would Trudeau go to limit freedom during the crisis? "Just watch me."

But when Trudeau tried to change the CBC by installing his colleague and crony Pierre Juneau as president, Juneau could do nothing about the increasingly adversarial attitude of the CBC programmers toward government policy. Emboldened by the outcry over the murder of *This Hour* back in Pearson's time, the corporation built the nation's largest and most expensive engine of news and views. Today its current-affairs programs are decked out with enough self-hyping fanfare and synthesizer gimmickry to make an American network blush – all to hound politicians in office and to cultivate them as allies when they're out.

The corporation's "anti" attitude applies whatever party is in power. While it has yet to be tested with an NDP national government, my hunch is that the darts would keep on coming. Despite their union affiliations, reporters and commentators would surely find an NDP government as hard to countenance as one led by Tories or Grits.

The CBC notes that the networks carry more than 400 newscasts a day, plus a weekly total of 1,000 hours of other journalism. Nerves are sometimes pinched and toes trod upon, says the CBC, but to back away to avoid offence would betray the highest journalistic principles and mislead a public that increasingly depends on the electronic media.

The corporation line is that it implements its informational responsibilities with a care and sensitivity for accuracy, fairness, balance and thoroughness, and that this approach inevitably means that newsmakers will not always be shown as they wish to be.

In spite of which, the CBC did see the need to appoint one of its top mandarins to act as an independent arbiter of complaints with direct access to President Juneau. That was three years ago, and nothing has been heard of, or from, this official since.

Prime Minister Mulroney has despaired of getting an even chance in reaching the people who elected him. No different from other PMs before him, he has said he wishes he could avoid the CBC and go to the people directly. But there is no way, regardless of all the hordes of government flacks on call.

His suspicions are fed by the way questions are spun on leading CBC news review programs, notably *Morningside*, *As It Happens*, *The House*, and *Sunday Morning* on radio, and *The Journal* on television.

The CBC and other media do not have a monopoly on manipulation. One of the biggest manipulators of the news is the government itself.

The Canadian government employs more than a thousand public relations officers in Ottawa to "present" its news. All ministers and many MPs also have press officers.

Using these publicity resources, successive governments have tried to bypass supposedly non-partisan media channels such as the CBC, but without success. Pierre Trudeau created Information Canada out of a straightforward desire to communicate his policies to the electorate. When it became a critical disaster, he reluctantly extricated himself from it, while maintaining that it was a good idea.

Brian Mulroney tried something similar. He contracted Ken Lawrence's television propaganda service to carry his message across the country by satellite, for a fee. Lawrence lost his membership in the Parliamentary Press Gallery, which tries to fend off lobbyists and flacks (although it's a hard line to police, and one former Press Gallery president was known to be a party bagman. His name was Charles Lynch – no relation.)

While our prime ministers would prefer not to have anything to do with the Canadian media, there is one forum they all crave.

Without exception they yearn to hit the front pages of the *New York Times*.

Few have rated even a mention on page one. Such space as Canada can command is inside the paper; on Sunday, Canada usually rates no space at all.

To the great chagrin of Prime Minister Pearson, newly elected

Ottawa Mayor Charlotte Whitton not only got stories of her antics on page one, but there was a photo of her, too.

No Canadian prime minister has ever managed that.

The Times of London used to be the chosen vehicle of status for our PMs. (They had no desire to appear on the front page, however, as until recent decades that august journal printed only classifieds on page one.)

The Times of London had a correspondent in Ottawa virtually from the day of Confederation, and yet the Canadian dispatches seldom achieved prominence and were grouped with other tidings from the colonies.

Even after Canada's Roy Thomson bought *The Times* and introduced a touch of Timmins into its affairs, prime ministers of Canada fared poorly in its columns. Thomson was little disposed to remedy this, as it was Prime Minister Diefenbaker who refused to let him take the British viscountcy he had bought and paid for, leaving Thomson no alternative but to give up his Canadian passport to become a lord.

In latter years an additional problem for our prime ministers is ensuring that these papers keep their Ottawa bureaus open. Our governments continue the fight, because they know that if there is no special correspondent to report the news, the agency versions are unlikely to be printed at all. At the time of writing, both bureaus are in limbo.

We in the Parliamentary Press Gallery were touched when, back in 1970, *The Times* of London reversed its decision to fold its Ottawa bureau and instructed its correspondent, Hilary Brigstocke, to remain at his post.

The reversal, said *The Times*, was the result of "certain expressions of regret in Canada" made in diplomatic as well as editorial quarters, with the government of Pierre Trudeau taking a hand. *The Times* said that Brigstocke's job was "a small but important link, worth preserving."

Brigstocke was by far the most popular foreign

correspondent ever to serve in Ottawa; the news that he'd be staying on after all was good news indeed at the National Press Club. But I'm not sure that his additional term did anything except impair his health. Certainly his treatment by *Times* chairman Kenneth Thomson, who said he was preserving Brigstocke's position "for sentimental and personal reasons," contributed to his untimely death.

So, probably, did the 1971 royal tour of the north . . . .

On that occasion the entire royal press corps was stranded in Tuktoyaktuk by a disabled Hercules aircraft, and the royals proceeded without us. There was only one telephone line out of Tuktoyaktuk, and each of the fifty-odd correspondents present was allotted two minutes to get out a dispatch.

Brigstocke won the draw and went first, putting in his call to the London *Times* bureau in New York.

"Brigstocke here," he bellowed down the line.

"Who?"

"Brigstocke, you bloody idiot. Your man in Ottawa. I have a dispatch."

"Shoot."

"Dateline is Tuktoyaktuk."

"Huh?"

"Tuktoyaktuk, you fool. T-U-K-"

"T-U-what?"

"Tuk, dammit! As in fuck!"

"Spell, please."

"T-U-K-T-O-Y-A-K-T-U-K."

"Where, please?"

"Northwest Territories. Christ, I'm almost out of time."

"Go ahead."

"Tuktoyaktuk, Northwest Territories. The entire press corps accompanying Her Majesty the Queen was stranded without food, shelter, or sustenance–"

Click.

"Sorry, Brigstocke," broke in the voice of tour coordinator Col. James McPhee. "Time's up. Next."

"Oh, fuck," said Brigstocke.

I'm not sure he ever recovered.

The Times' Ottawa bureau went by the boards eventually, for all the brave efforts of our government and the dogged Brigstocke.

So without any foreign escape route to the big time, our Canadian PMs are stuck with our own media and their very own CBC – "Holy Mother Corp" in the lingo of us print journalists, "that goddam CBC" to every government.

15. The Preems and the Supremes

"Canada is a terribly difficult nation to govern. The only way to do it is through co-operative federalism, involving not brute strength but consultation and compromise with provincial governments."   — *Pierre Trudeau*

In all the world Canada has no known enemies.

But within the country the federal government has at least ten, and maybe twelve: the leaders of the provincial and territorial governments.

If looks could kill, most of our prime ministers would have terminated most of our premiers. And vice versa.

The notion of the provinces as equal partners is a comparatively recent one – you can bet it wasn't uppermost in the minds of the Fathers of Confederation when, largely inflamed by strong drink, they founded the country. (It's one of history's ironies that the federation in the United States of America began with the idea of strong state components and ended up with strong central government, whereas in Canada we began with the concept of strong central government and ended up with strong provinces.)

As with most things Canadian, the subject of premiers poses a language problem.

"Prime minister" translates into French as "premier ministre." That, in turn, translates back into English as "first minister."

Hence the compromise at federal-provincial conferences, where all heads of government, federal and provincial, are called first ministers, or *premiers ministres* in French.

Earlier in this century, the prime minister of Canada was called a premier, as was the prime minister of Britain. But gradually "premier" as a form of address applied to a national leader fell into disuse, first in London and later in Ottawa and the capitals of the other Commonwealth nations.

Then Jean Lesage, head of the provincial government of Quebec, demanded the title of prime minister whenever he was addressed in English.

After which John Robarts of Ontario also decided he wanted to be called prime minister and had the title stenciled on his office door.

And in British Columbia, W.A.C. Bennett announced that henceforth, if not forever, he should be called prime minister of his province.

Pearson said that he'd call the premiers anything except what he really thought of them.

The Canadian Press refused point-blank to call John Robarts prime minister, so "Premier Robarts" he remained in print, if not on his office door and his letterhead and documents and among his entourage. And though Quebec's Daniel Johnson continued Lesage's use of the prime minister title when speaking English (he let it be known that he would not answer any reporter or television interviewer who addressed him as "Mr. Premier"), still the word "premier" stuck as the title for provincial leaders and since 1960 has been standard usage throughout anglo Canada.

Whatever they were called, all provincial premiers made life miserable for all prime ministers.

One of the most unforgettable battles of this century was between Trudeau and Lévesque, with Trudeau *versus* the Rest as background music.

Joe Clark's fight with Tory premiers nearly drove him around the bend and certainly hastened his departure from office.

And Pearson versus Jean Lesage deserves a mention, marking as it did the Quiet Revolution in Quebec. I once saw Pearson literally tearing his hair over the unrelenting pressures from fellow Liberals Lesage, Lévesque and Gérin-Lajoie at the federal-provincial conference in Quebec City.

Both Diefenbaker and Pearson *versus* Joey Smallwood were events worth watching – Smallwood treated any visiting federal politician as a doormat.

Yet the most poisonous relationship between a PM and a premier in Canadian history was that between Mackenzie King and Ontario's Mitchell Hepburn, fifty years back.

Both were Liberals, but their running feud, marked by Hepburn's alliance with Quebec's Union Nationale and Alberta's Social Credit against the central authority, was as near as we have come to a fascist-style revolution.

Mitchell Hepburn was short and bald, with a rolling gait and eyes that seemed to smile when his mouth didn't. He was known as a womanizer and a drinker, and enjoyed the company of assorted barons of Bay Street.

When he came to office at the age of thirty-eight in 1934, he immediately put into effect draconian economic measures: pay cuts for Ontario's elected members and civil servants, the closing of several provincial government offices and the auctioning off, in Toronto's Varsity Stadium, of the previous Tory government's forty-seven automobiles, including former premier George S. Henry's Packard limousine.

Among the messages of congratulation he received for his fist-swinging arrival on the scene was Mackenzie King's wish to see the Ontario premier "in public life for the next fifty years." King would heartily recant when Hepburn became Canada's answer to Louisiana's Huey Long.

During a series of disputes with his federal counterparts Hepburn gradually broke the provincial party organization away from the federal branch in Ontario. He even contemplated abolishing provincial party lines altogether and combining the Liberal and Conservative parties in an anti-Ottawa coalition. In this he was egged on by the *Globe and Mail's* George McCullagh, the archetypal North American fascist of the 1930s.

Hepburn espoused open associations – and hidden ones, too – with the business and industrial tycoons of his time, and in defence of their interests he became a union buster. Like his boozing buddy Duplessis of Quebec and Alberta's bible-thumping, prohibitionist Social Credit Premier Aberhart, he was impatient with democracy and convinced that there must be an easier way to run a country.

Hepburn exploited his allies when it suited him, caring little for Alberta's or Quebec's concerns except when these coincided with his obsession to undermine the nefarious feds. Mackenzie King, said Hepburn, was as useful to the nation as mustard plaster on a wooden leg. When hostilities with Nazi Germany escalated, Hepburn rose in the Ontario legislature to say that King had not done his duty to his country– . . . never has and never will." He introduced a resolution regretting that the federal government had made so little effort to prosecute Canada's duty in the war "in the vigorous manner the people of Canada desire to see."

The resolution passed forty-four to ten, the ten being dissident members of Hepburn's own party.

Before the Americans came into the war, Hepburn proclaimed the United States to be swarming with Nazi sympathizers and called on the able-bodied men of Ontario to act for the protection of their homes, factories, wives and children.

"I have no confidence in the Dominion government being of help to us in the event of such an invasion of our fair province," he said. He then banned an American documentary film called *Canada at War* from Ontario screens on the grounds that it was blatant propaganda for King.

Ottawa called his actions hysteria. Air Minister C.G. "Chubby" Power, a friend of Hepburn's, said that the Ontario premier had gone crazy.

In the middle of all this, Prime Minister King recorded in his diary the rumor that the forty-three-year-old Hepburn was sick and dying. "I believe it would be the most fortunate thing that could happen at this time," King wrote.

But the rumor was only half true. There was plenty of fire in Mitch Hepburn's belly yet. When he recovered he turned his attention to King's proposed plebiscite on military conscription for overseas service. Hepburn labeled the proposal "the most dastardly, contemptible, and cowardly thing ever perpetrated on a respected and dignified country by any government." He declared the King government a sham and King himself an appeaser.

Hepburn's frenzied harassment of Ottawa carried on throughout the war. He intervened for the Tories in the federal by-election that pitched Arthur Meighen, resurrected as federal leader of the Conservative Party, against schoolteacher Joseph Noseworthy of the CCF.

Meighen lost by 4,500 votes. Mackenzie King rejoiced. Referring to Hepburn, he said, "There never was such treachery on the part of a leader of a government towards another government supposed to be of the same political stripe." Something "vile and bad" had been defeated, he said.

When Hepburn abruptly resigned as premier and leader of the Liberal Party, he claimed to be unwilling to kowtow to Ottawa. The real reason was that Mitch Hepburn could no longer cope: he was short of money and supporters and long on whiskey.

After stepping down, he sat as provincial treasurer, and sniped as best he could at King and Ottawa. But he was in decline, and he took the Ontario Liberal Party with him. In the 1943 provincial election the Liberal Party won only fourteen seats, the beginning of forty-three years of Tory government in Ontario. "The men who had any association with Hepburn were doomed," wrote Mackenzie King. "In my inner nature I feel a sense of relief that a cabinet that has been so unprincipled and devoid of character has been cleaned out of Queen's Park."

Cleaned right out of town, in fact. Hepburn lived his remaining years on his onion farm where, in 1953, at age fifty-six, he died.

From the Preems to the Supremes.

Dealing with the Supreme Court has become a critical part of the prime minister's job since the advent of Canada's Charter of Rights and Freedoms. In any legislation that involves the charter, the court has to be taken into account. A prime minister can still appoint Supreme Court judges, but his freedom of choice is increasingly restricted, and one day soon constitutional change may do away with it entirely.

Not so long ago Canadians saw little national significance in the operation of their Supreme Court. The activities of the court went largely unreported, and the judges themselves were only on public view together at the opening of Parliament.

When I first witnessed this august group in the Senate chamber during those ceremonies, they were perched perilously on the woolsack, an absurd, old, moth-eaten hassock borrowed from the traditions of Britain.

In those day the judges were a world unto themselves. They dined together at the sedate Rideau Club, their table forbidden to other members.

They also fished together at the Magannassippi Fish and

Game Club, four hours by road and ferry northwest of Ottawa, in the wilds of Quebec.

One time, four of the Supremes were driving home from their fishing jaunt when their car was stopped by an officer of the Ontario Provincial Police. The officer had reason to believe that the driver and his passengers had been drinking.

When the judges revealed their identities, the cop called headquarters for instructions, which were: tell their lordships to drive carefully. And get out of there as fast as he could.

Times change.

In 1973, two days after Christmas, Prime Minister Trudeau appointed Bora Laskin chief justice of Canada, a move that forever destroyed the insularity of the judges.

The appointment was a public humiliation for the man who was in line for the top job – Mr. Justice Ronald Martland. As a sixteen-year veteran of the court from Alberta, he was the logical choice in succession to Chief Justice J.R. Cartwright. (Laskin had been a member of the court for only three years, and at age sixty-two he was five years Martland's junior.) That Martland was passed over was seen as a blow not just to him personally but to the legal profession in western Canada.

But Trudeau was envisaging a day when his cherished charter of rights would be enacted into law, and the court would become an integral part of the governing process, even if this meant conceding some of the PM's power.

Whereas critics decried the fact that Laskin's background in law was entirely academic, the academician Trudeau counted this a plus. In Laskin he saw brilliance, mental nimbleness and an appetite for reform.

Trudeau had confided his long-range plans to his appointee, and Laskin immediately began arousing public and media interest in the Supreme Court, preparing the way for developments to come.

Laskin was tireless in his lobbying of the national press corps for more and deeper coverage of his court. His place as a leading member of the Jewish community drew the public eye toward him and away from the old clannish court whose image he wished to change. His speeches had sparkle, and he went about his work with a jaunty air, shaking out the cobwebs in the marble halls and reactivating the moribund press room in the Supreme Court basement.

He barely lived to see the Charter of Rights and Freedoms become a reality. Indeed, it was felt that his work on the charter and the attendant legal complications hastened his death. But he knew that his work was a success and his duty fulfilled: he had put the Supreme Court squarely on the political map. Every Canadian prime minister would now have to seek the support of the Supreme Court and its chief justice in the making and administering of laws and policies affected by the charter.

Of all the men Pierre Trudeau worked with, Bora Laskin was the only one he revered. It was a feeling shared by everyone who knew him in the press corps, and Laskin's missionary work has been ably continued by his successor, Brian Dickson.

In addition to the responsibilities that the charter has brought to the chief justice, he still has to stand in for the governor-general (as Laskin did so tirelessly for the gravely ill Jules Léger) and administer the selection of candidates for the Order of Canada, which Laskin considered his most vexing task.

Since the choice of chief justice still lies with the prime minister of the day, the Order of Canada award is open to the charge that a "fix" is possible, especially since three other members of the Advisors Council that draws up the honors list are government appointees. But there's been no evidence of any collusion so far. The one stink to date came when author Morley Callaghan refused an Officer-level award because fellow author Hugh MacLennan had been made a top-level Companion. That was pique, though, not politics, and Callaghan got his Companionship eventually.

The fact that I received an order, in 1977, is proof that the prime minister carries little weight with the Advisory Council.

To this day mine remains the only Order of Canada bestowed on an active member of that thorn in the PM's side, the Parliamentary Press Gallery. I'm told I got it for my harmonica playing.

For all their traditional duties, today's Supreme Court judges are a far cry from their mostly anonymous predecessors. Their appointments are now widely noted and commented upon, and their records, either in politics or on the bench, are discussed with at least some of the fervor that accompanies Supreme Court nominations in the United States.

In some ways the judges are more powerful than the prime minister. Together they have the authority under the charter to strike down the law. And they don't have to face the electorate.

Like senators, Supreme Court judges can stay on until the mandatory retirement age of seventy-five. Or they can take early retirement and, if they are Willard Estey, spend the rest of their days sounding off against the Meech Lake Accord, against Ottawa as Moscow North, and against fellow judges as whiners.

Such extracurricular blasts may be the least that PMs can expect from our new age of involved Supremes.

16. The Royal We

"As useless as teats on a bull."   – *Senator Harry Hays*

Governors-general are supposed to symbolize the nation-state above and beyond partisan politics. They exist to provide sage advice and otherwise act as counselors and guides to our prime ministers, who are, in turn, the GG's principal advisers.

But no governor-general has ever been of the slightest assistance to any prime minister in the governance of this country, and no prime minister has ever rendered any help to a governor-general in the role of head of state.

The fact remains, however, that ever since the white man came to our shores, Canada has been a monarchy – first French, then English – and a prime minister must defer to a governor-general as the representative of a crowned head who is superior to everyone.

As we are stuck with this archaic arrangement, it's a pity that the setup isn't fun, as it used to be when the Brits sent eccentrics over to Rideau Hall.

But a closer look at some of the governors-general of my working lifetime reveals variety, at least.

Our first Canadian governor-general was Vincent Massey, one of the most anglicized men in the country. He even made British toffs feel inferior. He was appointed by Louis St. Laurent, and the two men actually succeeded in having a working relationship, probably because both of them were so strong on observing the formalities and both were Grits.

Massey is looked back on as a bridge between the end of colonialism and the emergence of our independence. He chaired a royal commission that attempted to describe Canada's identity, and much that has since affected and afflicted our culture, such as the Canada Council and the complex of arts subsidies, stemmed from those volumes.

For all he was fond of pomp and circumstance, Massey wore the Liberal label, and Diefenbaker couldn't wait to get rid of him when the Tories came to power in 1957.

Diefenbaker's choice was Georges Vanier, the first Quebecker to hold the highest office and the first GG to say it was possible to be a loyal Canadian without supporting the Crown.

Vanier's relations with the man who appointed him quickly became cold and formal, for Diefenbaker grew jealous of Vanier's stature in the country (just as Trudeau would later become jealous of Roland Michener's high profile).

Diefenbaker averaged a mere five visits a year with his GG, including such formal get-togethers as advising a dissolution of Parliament. In one year, 1960, there is no record of any visit at all from the PM, and that was the year the Tory government started to come apart – a time when a prime minister might be expected to want someone to talk to in his moments of stress.

And what was Vanier doing while "his" government was going down the drain?

He was subjecting himself to the torments and torrents of anguished prayer.

According to the eye-opening biography by his son, Jean, the governor-general began his day at Rideau Hall, as he had every day throughout his career in the military and in diplomacy, with an hour of contemplative prayer. Day's end found him in the chapel, "close to the altar in the presence of God." In the hours between there was the celebration of mass, and many other visits to the chapel besides.

As the prime minister's career was going to hell in a handbasket, Vanier was visiting the shrine of Bernadette at Lourdes. From Vanier's diary we learn that his pilgrimage to Lourdes was "an act of faith, in recognition and thanks for all the supernatural help that has been given me since I am Governor General."

Diefenbaker, though a devout Baptist, would have had trouble understanding the intensity of Vanier's spiritual feelings had he known their full extent. The public's only clue to the overpowering nature of their governor-general's faith was that he had once chastised a soldier who blasphemed in the midst of a bayonet battle in the First World War. (Vanier lost a leg in that fight.)

His religiosity was no inhibition to his friendship with Pearson, his former subordinate in diplomatic service. On Pearson's succession as prime minister in 1963 the visits between prime minister and governor-general increased dramatically, until they were occurring every ten days or so.

Vanier died in office, and his successor was Roland Michener, named by Pearson in the face of utter scorn from the leader of the opposition.

Michener was a lifelong Tory, but as speaker of the House of Commons he fell out with Diefenbaker when Tories suspected he was favoring opposition MPs in order to counter their big majority. When Michener lost his seat, he was cast into the political outer regions until Pearson won power and named him high commissioner to India, where the politics were laundered out of him – not a bad thing to happen to a future GG.

Michener and Pearson were comfortable with each other, but Trudeau had no time for governors-general. He didn't give a damn about the British Crown and its vice-regal trappings, and he said so in public. What tolerance he had of the monarchy was only out of respect for those who did care about it. Such people would disappear with the century, he said.

His main concern about Roly Michener was the amount of public attention the man was getting. He begrudged published photos of Michener jogging, swinging from ropes and smashing tennis balls – things associated with the new prime minister, not with a denizen of Rideau Hall. Meanwhile, Norah Michener deplored Trudeau's manners and sense of appropriate attire: buckskins when making formal calls at Rideau Hall and sandals, slacks, sports shirt and ascot – and usually an outrageous hat – for her garden parties.

Although Trudeau started out in office regarding governors-general as he did senators (and, indeed, the opposition members of the House of Commons) as "nobodies," his appointment of Jules Léger to succeed Michener seemed to indicate he had a serious purpose in mind.

The most scholarly of our GGs, Léger applied himself to the job as though it mattered and proceeded to make a series of speeches redefining the Canadian political and social scene, past and present.

In the beginning he was as utterly and openly indifferent to the Crown as his PM was. To Léger the office of governor-general was an entirely Canadian institution, greatly in need of heavy injections of the French language and culture, and he was repelled by the ceremonial side of his duties.

He had a tendency to speak out on the issues of the day. His views on non-political topics were often far more interesting than the usual governors-generalities.

Canadians were just beginning to come to terms with a governor-general who said meaningful things, when Léger was felled by a stroke. He was rendered virtually mute for the rest of his tenure, with the consequence that the presence of his office was minimized. This seemed to suit Trudeau very well. At any rate, Trudeau did nothing to encourage Léger's retirement.

A small irony in the story of this French representative of an English monarch is that when he made a partial recovery of his powers of speech, it was only his French that returned. His once-polished English was almost completely gone, to the point where he and the Queen spoke and communicated only in French. The Queen thanked him for this, "because since General de Gaulle you are the first person to speak to me regularly in French. . . it gives me practice."

Reversing his lifelong indifference to the British monarchy, Léger now professed respect and affection for Her Majesty the Queen, referring to her in his farewell speech as *"ma reine à moi"* – my own queen.

After Léger came Trudeau's trick on the Tories – his appointment of Ed Schreyer, just before Joe Clark was elected prime minister. With all his other problems, Clark had no time for a former NDP premier of Manitoba turned governor-general.

When Trudeau returned to office, he found Schreyer amusing at first. In Schreyer's earlier incarnation as Manitoba's premier Trudeau had thought him a kindred soul. But Trudeau soon grew bored with him and was happy to have him keep a low profile.

Schreyer brought the office of governor-general down to earth with a bump. And that's all he did with the job, for he lacked the stimulating common touch of some of his socialist peers in Britain. He was the youngest GG ever, and tended to hide behind the flamboyance of his bouncy wife, Lily. He spent his spare time in the country's dullest government job reading the *Encyclopaedia Britannica* from end to end and taking up soapstone carving.

At the end of Schreyer's term Trudeau had a problem finding another role for him. Finally he sent him to Australia, and no more was heard of him apart from a brief flurry about something reactionary he said concerning homosexuals on one of his many visits to his beloved Manitoba.

Trudeau's next trick on the Tories was to saddle them with Jeanne Sauvé.

Sauvé's appointment as governor-general was hailed, for she was the first woman in the job, and she had become a success as speaker of the House of Commons after a disastrous start.

She was a lifelong Grit, but her years in the speaker's chair were said to have scrubbed some of the partisanship out of her. Her husband, Maurice, however, a former minister in the Pearson cabinet and one of the few Quebeckers to oppose Trudeau's candidacy at the Liberal leadership convention of 1968 was, and remains, as partisan as ever. If Trudeau wanted revenge on Maurice Sauvé, he got it by naming Mme. Sauvé to Rideau Hall and sentencing Maurice to being her escort, a parody of Dennis Thatcher or Prince Philip. When he sought the directorship of Heritage Canada, he was howled down.

Jeanne Sauvé came to office suffering from a critical throat ailment that might have silenced her as completely as Léger. But she recovered, with only a rasp in her voice as evidence of what she'd gone through. She then put on airs and built walls around herself and her office that had not been there before.

Mulroney has made only token efforts to establish relations with Jeanne Sauvé, and he delivered an open insult to her by not inviting her to the Shamrock Summit with President Reagan, held in Quebec City. The excuse was that Reagan's was a working rather than a state visit, which didn't stop either man from treating it as a major photo and singsong opportunity.

Neither Sauvé nor Mulroney seems inclined to play the game, and in the Canadian context the game has become meaningless.

Modern governors-general don't really represent the Queen at all, no matter how regularly Sauvé protests that she writes to Her Majesty. And it's unlikely that Mulroney will ever be inclined to consult with the Queen, either directly or through her viceroy. All his instincts lean toward the United States, and the many Quebec Tories don't give a damn about the Queen and never will.

I miss England. It took a lot of our history with it when we cut it adrift. Its presence used to loom large in Canada, and during the last war there were even plans to move the British government to Canada, monarchy and all, if Britain fell to Hitler.

When I first came to Ottawa in 1947, the Canadian government telephone book had twenty pages of entries for the British High Commission, and I remember thinking that this was the most natural thing in the world.

But a big change started after Mackenzie King. In 1956, during the Suez Crisis, Prime Minister St. Laurent found himself offering Her Canadian Majesty advice directly opposed to the advice she was getting from her British prime minister, Sir Anthony Eden.

In the midst of that same crisis our PM found himself compromised by the very mention of British monarchy. I shall never forget standing beside Lester Pearson when he was making one of his many calls from the United Nations to St. Laurent that fateful week. Pearson was briefing his prime minister on the final stages of the Canadian initiative to put a UN emergency force in the Middle East to prevent further hostilities, following the attack on Egypt by Britain and France.

Suddenly Pearson slapped his forehead and groaned. "Oh, no!" he said. "Not the Queen's Own, for heaven's sake!"

St. Laurent had just told him that the Canadian regiment of that name was ready to embark for Egypt. Pearson knew very well that a regiment called the Queen's Own Rifles would make the Egyptians hit the roof.

St. Laurent stood his ground, but in the end the Canadian contingent did not include the Queen's Own.

If the British influence is behind us, there is a great deal of it I cherish. Our two best governors-general were Brits – John Buchan (Lord Tweedsmuir), the author of *The Thirty-Nine Steps* and other classic suspense yarns, who brightened the Depression with his wit and understanding; and the war hero Field Marshal Viscount Alexander of Tunis. Both men had world reputations. (We almost got Field Marshall Montgomery of Alamein, but "Monty" snorted his refusal when told the post held no authority.)

In recalling such Britons as these, it's worth pointing out that Quebeckers are determined to remember the French governors of New France who occupied the office before the British or Canadians ever came to do so. When Jules Léger was governor-general, he had the names of every French governor of New France carved on the wall of Rideau Hall, and most Quebec schoolchildren can recite these names by heart.

English-speaking students know nothing of governors-general, unless their school happens to be named after one, or unless the Stanley or Grey cups are being contested.

17. Capital Appreciation

"I have never understood why Queen Victoria chose a national capital filled with civil servants."

– Supreme Court Justice Willard Estey

Ottawa has taken on new sparkle with each passing year. Yet those of us who live here still find ourselves apologizing for the place, on the assumption that Canadians who live elsewhere feel scorn for their capital.

Ottawa has a history of being damned, not least of all by our prime ministers.

The only two PMs who really liked Ottawa were Mackenzie King and Pearson, and both preferred the nearby Gatineau Hills to the city itself. (It was those same hills that saved Pierre Trudeau from loathing Ottawa entirely.)

R.B. Bennett lived in a hotel throughout his prime ministry, and Louis St. Laurent lived, for a while anyway, in an apartment house.

Madame St. Laurent tried staying in the apartment with her husband, storing preserves and jams under the bed, but finally she retreated to the capacious family mansion on Quebec City's Grande Allée and turned the job of prime ministerial consort over to her daughters.

Uncle Louis had no apparent quarrel with apartment living, and when he moved to 24 Sussex Drive – the first prime minister to occupy that former Australian High Commission – he did so under protest and insisted on paying rent.

Diefenbaker pretended to like Ottawa, but he rarely involved himself in its social life after his gregarious early days as an MP. He was the last prime minister to walk the streets of the city, confining his later rambles to the lanes and byways of his posh Rockcliffe neighborhood or to the ceremonial expanse of Sussex Drive and Wellington Street.

The residents of Rockcliffe have always preferred diplomats and mandarins to politicians, and they raised an unholy howl after Diefenbaker's death when there was talk that his house might become a museum. It might attract crowds, they protested. Now that embassies have become fortresses, parts of Rockcliffe resemble an armed camp.

Pearson liked Ottawa because he had no other home after his diplomat's years abroad and a childhood spent in assorted parsonages all over western Ontario. Ottawa was where the power was, behind those green baize doors that give the old East Block corridors their look of rows of upended billiard tables.

Pearson was so at home in the Gatineau Hills just north of the city that he chose to be buried there. He is one of only three prime ministers whose graves are in the capital area. (The others are Borden and Laurier.)

None of the prime ministers have really known much about the life and soul of Ottawa, Brian Mulroney least of all. He, alone among prime ministers, never lived or worked in Ottawa before being elected party leader and then PM.

When Mulroney became prime minister, he hinted at the awful possibility of establishing his government's home-away-from-home in Baie Comeau. The prospect of frequent forays into the deep Quebec boonies was horrifying to Mulroney's cabinet, so the project was dropped. Mulroney put a penitentiary in his riding instead – our gain in accessibility being the convicts' loss.

Until Trudeau's time, prime ministers seldom went out on the town because there wasn't much town to go out on. The only decent restaurant was Madame Burger's in Hull, tucked behind the woodpile of the Eddy mill with its great neon sign advertising White Swan toilet paper.

When I came to Ottawa in 1947, it was a sleepy, English-speaking hicktown with ramshackle French enclaves. The snow in the streets was shoveled into horse-drawn sleds, leaving enough still on the ground for the sleighs of the well-to-do, who rode by swathed in huge raccoon coats and hats.

Only forty years ago this now-sleek city still had 480 outhouses and 350 railroad crossings. Sparks Street was the ugliest main street imaginable, and the downtown Rideau Canal was neglected. Smoke and soot were everywhere, mixed with the effluvium of Hull's pulp mills across the river.

There were no highrises, shopping malls were unknown and supermarkets were just starting to appear. Superhighways didn't exist either, and there was only the faint beginning of a parkway system.

Hull was sin city. The drinks and the women had not yet been replaced by autoroutes, bridges, and government buildings. (The citizens of Hull responded to this development by making their city a bastion of Quebec separatism.)

Ottawa the lumber town has recently transformed itself into one of the most attractive, the most striking, the most fun-to-live-in capital cities in the world.

Scarcely a feature of the old place is recognizable today, apart from Parliament Hill. And virtually the only uncluttered view of Parliament is to be had from the Quebec side of the Ottawa River.

Over there the old Eddy woodpile has been replaced by the strangest and most wonderful of all Canada's modern structures – Douglas Cardinal's curvaceous and utterly astonishing Museum of Civilization.

Within Ottawa's newness, a couple of its older buildings look better than ever. Demolition experts had their eye on the abandoned railway terminus in the heart of the city, and plans were in the works to transport some of its stone columns to Kingsmere to augment Mackenzie King's ruins. But wiser minds prevailed, and the old railway station became the government conference center. There the deal was hatched that patriated the constitution and devised the amending formula and the Charter of Rights and Freedoms.

Amid the blocks of glass that make downtown Ottawa resemble a pod of drifting icebergs, the Supreme Court building sits serene, the most handsome structure in town. It's not as Disneyesque as the Château Laurier or as Presbyterian Gothic as the Parliament buildings, but it's the very model of what a hall of justice should be, and its massive green copper top in the French-provincial style (Mackenzie King's idea) caps its perfection. If I were going to be sentenced by a court, I would want it to happen in these surroundings.

Mackenzie King was the planner of the modern Ottawa, and the physical changes he set in motion here have had almost as profound an effect on the image of the capital as the cultural revolution begun by Pearson and Trudeau and carried forward by Clark and Mulroney.

According to King's timetable, the future was where we are today. His master plan for handsome buildings connected by a system of parks and parkways was meant to be completed by the 1980s. King's dream stands all around us now. Whatever the new generations are taught about this man, they will be able to see with their own eyes the physical evidence of his high hopes for Canada's capital region.

At the heart of King's vision, only twelve minutes from downtown Ottawa, is Kingsmere. Tall, first-growth white pines are still extant here, spared the axes and saws that destroyed the forests of the Ottawa and Gatineau River valleys. Scattered about the area are surviving examples of the many summer homes built by Ottawa society at the turn of the century and before, when the way to Kingsmere was by train and stagecoach. People dressed for dinner in the homes of Kingsmere then, and their gardeners created settings that could have been transplanted from Edwardian England.

Willie King was regarded as an intruder, particularly after he started assembling parcels of property at bargain prices. But it was King who put to flight assorted developers and scotched their plans to create a resort suburb in the hills around Kingsmere. Ultimately, King's estate became the nucleus of Gatineau Park, his principal bequest to the nation. Without King those hills would have been alive with the sound of jackhammers for years.

The properties on his estate were in disrepair when King passed them along to the nation, and massive refurbishing has been necessary. The house in which King died, known as the Farm, was in such bad shape that when it was made the official residence of the speaker of the House of Commons, Alan Macnaughton had to spend $40,000 of his own money to make residency endurable. Subsequent speakers have forked out more private and public money, topped by $450,000 in government funds during the short regime of John Bosley. All speakers have reported signs of King's spiritual presence, though the plaque on the bed where he died was removed years ago because it frightened the children of Mr. Speaker Lucien Lamoureux.

I treasure the memory of the twenty summers I spent at my

cottage on the shores of Kingsmere, with its towering pines and its clear water. Visitors flock to Kingsmere today, sometimes 5,000 on a Sunday, driving the parkways and thronging the lookouts on the edge of the Laurentian Shield where it abruptly gives way to the Ottawa valley and the Laurentian Plain beyond.

There is scarcely any human habitation between Gatineau Park and the north pole. The bears wander and the deer roam freely. The owls nest and the ospreys soar overhead.

One of the big threats the prime minister of Canada faces from the electorate is the possibility that it will throw him out of his Harrington Lake summer domain and repossess the place for the people.

The 4,000-acre Harrington Lake estate in the Gatineau Hills is a major perk of the PM's job, and when the National Capital Commission suggested to Trudeau that maybe he'd like to deed the place over as a public park and establish the prime minister's summer residence somewhere more suitable for single-family use, he told them to go jump in another lake.

Trudeau then settled in for the duration and persuaded the custodians who oversee the estate to install and cultivate all the organic gardens that his "earth mother" Margaret would ever need. And when those same custodians sought to remove a tree on the property without consulting him, Trudeau stood in front of the bulldozer blade and said that the driver would have to kill him first.

Prime ministers are not always the easiest neighbors for residents of the Gatineau Hills. On the rare occasions that Trudeau himself drove his Mercedes 300SL along the road leading to Harrington Lake, it was at a speed that imperiled children, dogs and cats. Finally, for his own safety, the Mounties made him put his toy away in a garage, where he maintained it as meticulously as his bankroll.

Other menaces to the peace of the region are the limos and security vehicles that go with a PM's presence, and the helicopter that brought President Lyndon Johnson in for his 1967 visit. Then there's all the police security, which started when John Diefenbaker loaned the estate to Princess Margaret for her tryst with the young John Turner and tried to keep the press away.

The road that Trudeau roared along to his retreat runs past Meech Lake and two great country mansions that were spared the wrecker's ball when they were acquired as part of the national park. The larger of these mansions became a meeting place for ministers and premiers, and it was here that the federal government and other provinces agreed to recognize Quebec as a distinct society in exchange for Robert Bourassa's signature on the Constitution.

Some of the meetings that led to Quebec's signature were held in the downtown building known as the Langevin Block, and when final agreement was reached, there was talk of calling it the Langevin Accord. But Sir Hector Langevin was one of the greatest scoundrels ever to hold high office in Canada. So the decision was to go with the name of old Asa Meech.

Asa Meech was a New Englander respected in the Ottawa valley as a clergyman, farmer, teacher, and physician. He fathered six children by his first wife, Mary, and five more by her sister, Maria. Three of the first lot and Mary drowned in Hull's Brewery Creek when a bridge washed out. The tragedy was said to have turned Meech's hair white overnight. His third wife, Margaret, had ten children by him. Two of Meech's grandsons drowned in Meech Lake in 1883. A granddaughter married into the Harrington family, for whom the next lake in the Gatineau chain is named.

Stern Asa didn't know much joy in his seventy-four years, and his tombstone at Old Chelsea, on the way to Meech and Harrington lakes, bears the inscription:

"I would not live always, I ask not to stay, Where storm after storm rises dark o'er the way."

As a bit of political prophecy, that's not bad.

18. Fail Safe

"Why blame me for this mess?"   — *Mackenzie King*

I remember the day in 1966 when caucus chairman Bryce Mackasey burst out of a secret conclave, boasting that Pearson was the greatest prime minister the country had ever had.

The Pearson government was coping with assorted scandals that day, so I asked Mackasey if any members of the caucus had expressed dissatisfaction with the leader.

Mackasey replied: "The bond between him and the members of the caucus might be described as mystical."

"Sorry," I said. "Might be described as what?"

"Mystical," said Mackasey.

"A mystical bond?"

"Yes," said Mackasey. "A mystical bond. We all want him to stay."

Mackasey smiled when I confronted him a little later with the dictionary definition of mystical, which is:

"Of hidden meaning, mysterious; awe-inspiring; seeking by contemplation and self-surrender to obtain union with or absorption into the Deity or believing in spiritual apprehension of truths beyond the understanding."

"It could be all those things," said Mackasey, and he rejected my suggestion that maybe Mystical Bond was the sister of James and Israel.

As it was with Mackasey, so it is with all ministers. They insist that if only I could hear the prime minister in caucus, I would be amazed. The nation would marvel!

Evidently, prime ministers can cast spells in caucus that flop elsewhere. Why not open the caucus and let the press and the nation see them at their best? No, no. Caucus is where MPs and prime ministers get to speak their minds, stuff too strong for public consumption. The media has to make do with caucus leaks, which are not always as juicy as mystical bonds.

Much as the government of the day wants us to give its leader a decent hearing, it hides the real story from us and is then upset when media presume the prime minister guilty until proven otherwise. The prime minister that the nation sees and hears and reads about is scrambled and reinterpreted by whatever medium is doing the reporting.

No prime minister can have a fair hearing this way, nor would anybody in media concede that a PM is entitled to one.

Michel Gratton was a top-flight political reporter when Mulroney hired him. Gratton's 1987 book, *So What Are the Boys Saying?* was a compendium of mistakes committed by the prime minister, not the least of which was his hiring of Gratton to be press secretary. In the last chapter Gratton thanks Mulroney for accepting his resignation, thus "giving me back my life."

The book suggests to me that there ought to be a law banning journalists from politics, either as flacks or as elected members. It was Norman DePoe who said that journalists entering politics were like horse players who wanted to be horses.

Occasionally the thing works out the other way around – politicians become good journalists. Both Dalton Camp and Douglas Fisher have vicious streaks – valid tickets of admission to the media brigade. Neither covered a story in the true news sense, but Camp has style and Fisher remains an incurable snoop.

Worse than being a political reporter or a reporter turned press secretary is, to my mind, being a creature called the pollster. At least political reporters can say that they are animators of the political scene, drawing on experience of news gathering and presenting the news with some style that leads readers and listeners to think and decide for themselves. We say we don't tell people what to think but what to think about. (And then there's the one about comforting the afflicted, and afflicting the comfortable.)

But pollsters have cheapened the whole political process. Promoting the idea of policy by poll, they have disenchanted the populace and reduced elections to the mockery they were back when politicians bought votes with rum and two-dollar bills.

My remedy would be to limit pollsters' stuff to questions and answers and ban the sale of their interpretations, conclusions and recommendations as rigorously as we prohibit smoking in public places.

There are politicians who'd like to ban the interpretations, conclusions and recommendations of political journalists, as well.

Still, a few of us stay at it to the death, and it's perhaps worth noting that three sexagenarians in the trade – myself, Douglas Fisher, and George Bain – agree on one thing, namely that prime ministers don't get a square deal from the media.

So what *do* prime ministers get out of the job?

Disappointment, mostly.

Consider this, from Prime Minister Joe Clark:

"There is not much sex appeal in expenditure management. In fact, if the government wants to attract attention, it can ignore expenditure control. Then it will become known for the money it wastes. We would prefer to be known for the public money we save."

Four months later Clark and his government were defeated on a deficit-cutting budget, and Trudeau returned to head the highest-spending government in Canadian history.

One way to feel that you're on top of the crazy business of running this country is to let it run itself. That's what St. Laurent did, driving around in his Austin Princess limousine, letting the money and kudos roll in while the nation became Americanized.

There's always a day, or two, of reckoning. But if a PM can withstand the vicissitudes, the incidental rewards can be great.

R.B. Bennett's friendship with Max Aitken (Lord Beaverbrook) furnished him with a retirement gift of a peerage and title: Viscount Bennett of Mickleham, Calgary and Hopewell (a place in New Brunswick almost as remote as Aitken's Beaverbrook).

King and Borden got their physogs onto our paper money, King on the fifty-dollar bill and Borden on the hundred. When their faces first showed up on those banknotes, fifties and hundreds were scarcely in circulation, which moderated the supposed slight to Her Majesty, whose visage had been deemed essential to make our currency valid. Now the homely faces of Mackenzie King and Sir Robert Borden are everywhere.

Trudeau hasn't made it onto the money yet, but there's a lot that he must relish from his years in office. He ought to get a kick out of the way his presence changed our view of modern Canadian history. He distorts our view of the PMs before and since.

Legend blinds us to his failures. We remember Trudeau as a man always in control of himself, if not of his country or his wife. In fact, he dealt us a number of glancing blows.

Yet, Canada's growth and prosperity in modern times has

occurred in spite of all the real and imagined failures of its prime ministers, performing an increasingly impossible job.

I'll leave the last word to Trudeau:

"In this House and in every province in this country we are fighting to preserve a great and precious land. The most effective weapon we have is understanding. . .understanding and generosity towards each other's aspirations, as individuals, as members of cultural and regional communities – and as Canadians. . . .

"I know that the task for Canada will not be easy, but was it easy for the Canadians who settled a sometimes harsh land?

"Where they built with their hands and their heads, conquering nature, devising vast transportation systems, we must now build with our hearts."